ENGELS, ANGEL MEADOW AN

A TRUE ACCOUNT OF A MIGRANT IRISH F. ... IN ANGEL MEADOW

by

James Patrick Hynes

Copyright 2016 by James Patrick Hynes

Front Cover

The shamrock represents the Irish. Its blackening symbolises the poisonous industrial atmosphere endured by the people living in Angel Meadow. The young Engels was horrified by the abject poverty. He has been placed beneath the wrought iron gateway   which now marks the Meadow. On the right, policemen watch a notorious criminal jump into the filthy River Irk. An old archway passes under the railway viaduct showing a thief jumping out of a front door. An extract from a letter by a resident is shown.

CONTENTS

PREFACE

This account of a migrant Irish family living in Angel Meadow arose out of my reading through the family correspondence of John and Bridget Hynes, their children and friends when they lived in what contemporary commentators called: "The lowest, most filthy, most unhealthy, and most wicked locality in Manchester ..." Angel Meadow during the mid and late 19th-century. The letters are held by Ellen McCormick, of Ontario, Canada who is descended from John and Bridget's daughter Ellen Hynes and I am grateful to her my cousin, for encouraging me to use these letters in this short social history.

These letters along with my comments and various citations will contribute something towards representing the contextual reality of having to live and survive in a slum which housed the thousands of migrant people who worked the factories, foundries, gasworks and cotton spinning mills of a newly industrialised Manchester. They give a small voice to the suffering, the forgotten, the 'angels', and the devils, in Angel Meadow. It was once, one of the first open fields to be built upon during industrialisation of 'Cottonopolis', of Manchester the first great city of the Industrial Revolution. In days of yore about a hundred years previously Bonnie Prince Charlie's Jacobite Army had camped alongside the Irk and partook of the ale in the Angel Inn. The folksong, 'At the Angel Inn in Manchester' is said to date from then.

> **"It's coming down to Manchester to gain my liberty,**
> **I met a pretty young doxy and she seemed full of glee.**
> **Yes, I met a pretty young doxy, the prettiest ever I see.**
> **At the Angel Inn in Manchester, there is the girl for me."**

See the Appendix for the full ballad.

The river has long since been culverted so that today the murky brook disappears beneath Victoria railway station into a brick tunnel at Ducie Bridge emptying into another 'river', the Irwell, beneath a railway viaduct.

ORIGINS OF ANGEL MEADOW AND ST. MICHAEL'S FLAGS

Angel Meadow Park and St Michael's Flags, extending over 7.4 acres, are located in the immediate northeast of Manchester City Centre on a slope between the River Irk and Rochdale Road. Angel Meadow lay off the Oldham Road and was, in the nineteenth century, "… full of cellars and is inhabited by prostitutes, their bullies, thieves, cadgers, vagrants, tramps, and, in the very worst sites of filth, and darkness." Engels was so horrified by the place that it moved him into becoming a champion of the British working class along with his friend Karl Marx.

Today Angel Meadow is one of the few green spaces in Manchester's city centre close to the CIS tower, in the Northern Quarter within Ancoats and Clayton ward. Once a wealthy suburb of Manchester, the area was transformed during the industrial revolution into an appalling slum over- populated by migrants living in abject poverty and suffering dirt induced disease on the edges of Blake's Satanic Mills. It was there that the Irish immigrants, John (Hines) Hynes and Bridget Connolly, a very young widow, née Tierney, married, worked, raised their children and died early deaths. Although, as yet, we do not know what parts of Ireland they came from, we do know that John's surname was that of an illustrious Irish family, the Hynes, the O Heynes, or in Irish Gaelic Ui hEidhne whose history I have portrayed in my book The Hynes of Ireland.

The transformation of the rural landscape on the edges of Manchester took place between 1780 and 1790 as factories, foundries; gasworks and cotton spinning mills were built there. It was there in 1780 that Richard Arkwright began construction of Manchester's first cotton mill next to Angel Meadow transforming Manchester into the leader of the Industrial Revolution.

In 1788 an Anglican church called, St Michael's and All Angels was built as a carriage church for wealthy Mancunians driving from the town in that once gentrified part of Manchester but within twenty years a letter in the Manchester Guardian was asking, "Why one of the ugliest churches in Manchester situated in one of the most crowded and notorious parts of the City, should have so long enjoyed the pleasant sounding name 'St Michael's, Angel Meadow' is beyond understanding?" It was a neighbourhood in decline yet the church built by Humphrey Owen, a local benefactor, could seat just over a thousand people after it was consecrated on 23 July 1789.
Its new burial ground, the largest cemetery in Manchester, had already been consecrated by the Bishop of Chester and eventually used to bury or rather dispose of paupers who could afford neither funerals nor graves.

"There were two distinct classes of people living in this overcrowded hell hole. There were old established trustworthy families who were regarded as the salt of the parish. Then there were the drunken migrant settlers of the industrial revolution, dreaming of work in the big city of Manchester, but left brawling, fighting, drinking and indulging in 'unrestrained licentious womanising' in the grinding poverty of the slum trap zone. Mercle, probably Garlieb Mercle, a German writer and activist, pulled no punches in comparing the meadow to "a Serborian bog in sore need of draining'."

{Quotation from Friends of Angel Meadow on http://www.friends-of-angel-meadow.org/page26.htm}

"The real Angel Meadow was in one of the most notoriously squalid districts; there is a certain black irony to its name....'Anyone who knows Manchester', he says, 'can infer the adjoining districts from the appearance of the thoroughfare, but one is seldom in a position to catch from the street a glimpse of the real labouring districts'" {Ibid}

Certainly at the beginning of the 19th century poverty was regarded as the natural condition of the labouring poor due to harvest failures and the disruptions of war few ever blamed it upon people in power. The alleged generosity of outdoor relief was said to benefit the feckless and reduce the resources available to the deserving poor. That is an old story used to give the 'haves' an excuse to deprive the 'have-nots' of their just shares of the common good. A papal encyclical, 1967, Populorum Progressio (The Progress of People), Paul V reminded us that injustice causes poverty. Unjust structures uphold & foster dependency & poverty amounting to institutionalised violence. Poverty is caused by people.

1816 The Burial Ground

In the mid-19th century the population density of Angel Meadow was 350 persons per acre characterised by such a high death rate that the land adjacent to the church became the largest cemetery in Manchester used for the burials of people too poor to afford a proper funeral and between 1788 and 1816 more than 40,000 bodies were buried there in mass graves. The burial ground was then closed. Nevertheless, some of the more enterprising of the poor resorted to digging up Angel Meadow and selling its humus rich soil to nearby farmers as fertiliser. It took an Act of Parliament in 1855 to enable the municipality to cover it over with flagstones From then on it bore the name of St Michael's Flags. During the early 1860s a bare knuckle fight took place there and on that occasion when the bully 'Stumpy' bit completely through Bacup Billy's hand members of the crowd joined in and crushed Stumpy into a shapeless and bleeding mass. Billy died of his injuries the following year.

One principal feature of Angel Meadow is its proximity to the River Irk which flows through the northern suburbs of Manchester before joining the River Irwell in the city centre. Previously it has been known as the Iwrck or the Irke getting its name from a variant of the word for roe deer. In the Middle Ages there was a corn mill on its bank along with a fishery. Anyone standing at the top of that hillside until the late eighteenth century could have looked down on tree-lined lanes and a rusty-coloured river Irk teeming with trout and eels. Ancient hedgerows, including one that marked the future track of Angel Street, provided a haven for wildlife. The view across the river was unobstructed by slum housing or factory chimneys. A Victorian writer named Benjamin Redfern said this 'heavenly landscape' had 'one of the most beautiful views of vale and river, hill and woodland'. But all that changed as Angel Meadow became a slum. The river became a black watercourse covered in floating green slime, bubbling with stinking gases.

This sketch taken from the autobiography '25 Years of Detective Life – a fascinating account of crime in Victorian Manchester' by a famous Mancunian detective Jerome Caminada is as close as one can get to the appearance of the Irk in the late eighteenth century. It illustrates a time when a notorious brutal thieving blacksmith named Bob Horridge with policemen engaged in one of their frequent chases after him leapt into the Irk. "Down the steps that once formed an approach to Victoria Station by the footbridge Horridge rushed, bounding over the parapet into the filthy Irk, dashed along the river into the tunnel running underneath the Grammar School, Walker's Croft, and Hunts Bank, emerging at the junction of the waters into the River Irwell, until he came to a croft in Moreton Street, Strangeways, where he got clear away."

Caminada had little respect for the district in which he grew up and which he policed: "Then in Chester Street and Angel Meadow-not so much of a *meadow* now-and in a vicious streets around to which my thoughts are at the same time directed, 'the wicked never cease from troubling, nor were the weary even at rest', for their fitful midnight slumbers gave place, as daylight broke, to the restlessness of evil."

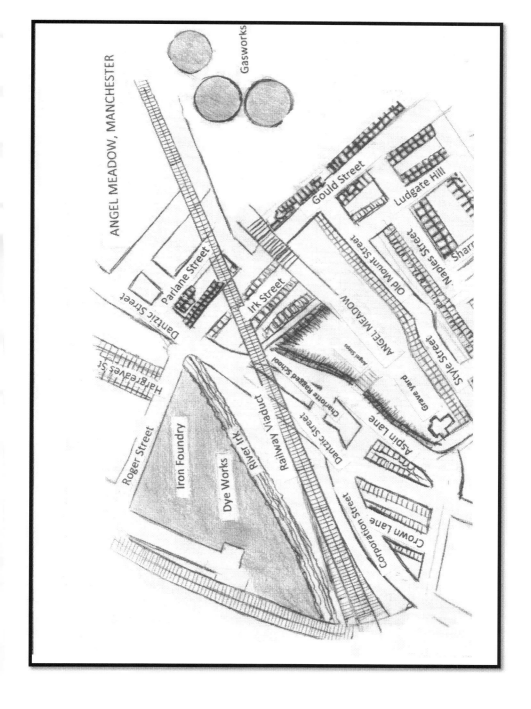

ANGEL MEADOW, MANCHESTER

Gasworks

Gould Street

Ludgate Hill

Sharp

Naples Street

Old Mount Street

ANGEL MEADOW

Style Street

Grove Yard

Angel Steps

Parlane Street

Irk Street

Dantzic Street

Halt Breaves St

Charlotte Ragged School

Dantzic Street

Aspin Lane

Roger Street

Iron Foundry

Dye Works

River Irk

Railway Viaduct

Crown Lane

Corporation Street

James Phillips Kay, Secretary to the Board of Health, had noticed that the rich, after moving out of the centre of Manchester lost sight of the poor leaving them unsupported without civic amenities. The shopkeepers, operators and labourers had to cope without adequate civic resources that we so take for granted now. It was said that the wealthy of Manchester knew less about Ancoats than they did about China! There were, as the politician Disraeli put it, two nations, the rich and the poor.

In the 1830s conditions were ripe for cholera to sweep throughout England's cities, towns and village, spread by contaminated food and drink and people on the move. In Manchester during the outbreak, 1325 people contracted the disease and 674 of them, died. In an attempt to cover up the bad smells barrels of tar and vinegar were burned in the streets but to avail.

Strange experiments involving dismemberment of victims were carried out in vain attempts to halt the spread of the disease. When the grandfather of a four year old victim John Brogan complained that there was no name on the coffin of his grandson, placed in an open pit Walker's Croft cemetery in Ancoats the coffin was opened and the headless body of corpse of the boy lay was revealed within.

Word of this mutilation spread through Irish Town asserting that doctors were killing Irish sufferers for experimentation. A mob then carried the coffin through the area to Swan Street shouting: "Burn the hospital!" The mob rioted, smashing the hospital windows and attacking staff. Apparently a medical student had in fact sawn off the child's head for research.

Kay's description of the area in 1832 is as terrible as any other of the descriptions already quoted. "The Irk, black with the refuse of dye works corrected on this bank, receives excrementitious matters from some sewers in this portion of the town-the drainage from gas works, and filth of the most pernicious character from the bone works, tanneries, size manufacturing these, and so on, immediately beneath Ducie-Bridge, in a deep hole between two high banks, its reach around a large cluster as some of the most wretched and dilapidated buildings of the town. The course of the River is here impeded by a Weir and a large tannery eight stories high (three of which stories are filled with skins exposed to the atmosphere, in some stage of the processes to which they are subjected) towers close to this crazy labyrinth of pauper dwellings. This group of habitations is called "Gibraltar," and no site can well be more insalubrious than that on which it is built." (**From The Moral and Physical Conditions of the Working Classes Employed in the Cotton Manufacture in Manchester by James Phillips Kay, MD, Manchester, 1832.)**

The City of Manchester became a place of enormous wealth nicknamed 'Cottonopolis' boasting impressive public and commercial buildings but also home to some of the nation's worst slums. After visiting Manchester in 1835, the French political thinker and historian, Alexis de Tocqueville, who thought Manchester to be anarchic , commented in his work <u>Journeys to England and Ireland</u>: 'From this foul drain the greatest stream of human industry flows out to fertilize the whole world. From this filthy sewer gold flows. Here humanity attains its most complete development and its most brutish, here civilization works its miracles and civilized man is turned almost into a savage.' His account also included a graphic description of the pauper burial ground at St. Michael's Flags.

1844, ENGELS WAS HORRIFIED BY THE PLACE

In 1842 Friedrich Engels , a German textile manufacturer, in an attempt to prise his son away from revolutionary activities and subversive writing sent young Friedrich to work at the family part owned cotton-factory Ermen & Engels, in 7 Southgate (the factory was in Weaste manufacturing patent cotton thread in Manchester. While there Friedrich was so shocked by the poverty in the city especially in Angel Meadow that some years later, using his personal observations and research, he wrote and published his great exposé The Condition of the Working Classes in England in 1844.

When describing the district of 'Irish Town' which included Angel Meadow, Engels wrote:

"The south bank of the Irk is here very steep and between fifteen and thirty feet high. On this declivitous hillside there are planted three rows of houses, of which the lowest rise directly out of the river, while the front walls of the highest stand on the crest of the hill in Long Millgate. Among them are mills on the river, in short, the method of construction is as crowded and disorderly here as in the lower part of Long Millgate. Right and left a multitude of covered passages lead from the main street into numerous courts, and he who turns in thither gets into a filth and disgusting grime, the equal of which is not to be found - especially in the courts which lead down to the Irk, and which contain unqualifiedly the most horrible dwellings which I have yet beheld. In one of these courts there stands directly at the entrance, at the end of the covered passage, a privy without a door, so dirty that the inhabitants can pass into and out of the court only by passing through foul pools of stagnant urine and excrement. This is the first court on the Irk above Ducie Bridge - in case anyone should care to look into it. Below it on the river there are several tanneries which fill the whole neighbourhood with the stench of animal putrefaction. Below Ducie Bridge the only entrance to most of the houses is by means of narrow, dirty stairs and over heaps of refuse and filth. The first court below Ducie Bridge, known as Allen's Court, was in such a state at the time of the cholera that the sanitary police ordered it evacuated, swept, and disinfected with chloride of lime. Dr. Kay gives a terrible description of the state of this court at that time. Since then, it seems to have been partially torn away and rebuilt; at least looking down from Ducie Bridge, the passer-by sees several ruined walls and heaps of debris with some newer houses. The view from this bridge, mercifully concealed from mortals of small stature by a parapet as high as a man, is characteristic for the whole district. At the bottom flows, or rather stagnates, the Irk, a narrow, coal-black, foul-smelling stream, full of debris and refuse, which it deposits on the shallower right bank". In dry weather, a long string of the most disgusting, blackish-green, slime pools are left standing on this bank, from the depths of which bubbles of miasmatic gas constantly arise and give forth a stench unendurable even on the bridge forty or fifty feet above the surface of the stream. But besides this, the stream itself is checked every few paces by high weirs, behind which slime and refuse accumulate and rot in thick masses. Above the bridge are tanneries, bone mills, and gasworks, from which all drains and refuse find their way into the Irk, which receives further the contents of all the neighbouring sewers and privies. It may be easily imagined, therefore, what sort of residue the stream deposits. Below the bridge you look upon the piles of debris, the refuse, filth, and offal from the courts on the steep left bank; here each house is packed close behind its neighbour and a piece of each is visible, all black, smoky, crumbling, ancient, with broken panes and window frames. The background is furnished by old barrack-like factory buildings. On the lower right bank stands a long row of houses and mills; the second house being a ruin without a roof, piled with debris; the third stands so low that the lowest floor is uninhabitable, and therefore without windows or doors. Here the background embraces the pauper burial-ground, the station of the Liverpool and Leeds railway, and, in the rear of this, the Workhouse, the "Poor-Law Bastille" of Manchester, which, like a citadel, looks threateningly down from behind its high walls and parapets on the hilltop, upon the working-people's quarter below.

"Above Ducie Bridge, the left bank grows more flat and the right bank steeper, but the condition of the dwellings on both banks grows worse rather than better. He who turns to the left here from the main street, Long Millgate, is lost; he wanders from one court to another, turns countless corners, passes nothing but narrow, filthy nooks and alleys, until after a few minutes he has lost all clue, and knows not whither to turn. Everywhere half or wholly ruined buildings, some of them actually uninhabited, which means a great deal here; rarely a wooden or stone floor to be seen in the houses, almost uniformly broken, ill-fitting windows and doors, and a state of filth! Everywhere heaps of debris, refuse, and offal; standing pools for gutters, and a stench which alone would make it impossible for a human being in any degree civilised to live in such a district. The newly-built extension of the Leeds railway, which crosses the Irk here, has swept away some of these courts and lanes, laying others completely open to view. Immediately under the railway bridge there stands a court, the filth and horrors of which surpass all the others by far, just because it was hitherto so shut off, so secluded that the way to it could not be found without a good deal of trouble. I should never have discovered it myself, without the breaks made by the railway, though I thought I knew this whole region thoroughly. Passing along a rough bank, among stakes and washing-lines, one penetrates into this chaos of small one-storied, one-roomed huts, in most of which there is no artificial floor scarcely kitchen, living and sleeping-room all in one. In such a hole five feet long by six broad, I found two beds - and such bedsteads and beds! - which, with a staircase and chimney-place, exactly filled the room. In several others I found absolutely nothing, while the door stood open, and the inhabitants leaned against it. Everywhere before the doors refuse and offal; that any sort of pavement lay underneath could not be seen but only felt, here and there, with the feet. This whole collection of cattle-sheds for human beings was surrounded on two sides by houses and a factory, and on the third by the river, and besides the narrow stair up the bank, a narrow doorway alone led out into another almost equally ill-built, ill-kept labyrinth of dwellings.... "

"If we leave the Irk and penetrate once more on the opposite side from Long Millgate into the midst of the working-men's dwellings, we shall come into a somewhat newer quarter, which stretches from St. Michael's Church to Withy Grove and Shude Hill. Here there is somewhat better order. In place of the chaos of buildings, we find at least long straight lanes and alleys or courts, built according to a plan and usually square. But if, in the former case, every house was built according to caprice, here each lane and court is so built, without reference to the situation of the adjoining ones.... "

" . . . Here, as in most of the working-men's quarters of Manchester, the pork-raisers rent the courts and build pig-pens in them. In almost every court one or even several such pens may be found, into which the inhabitants of the court throw all refuse and offal, whence the swine grow fat; and the atmosphere, confined on all four sides, is utterly corrupted by putrefying animal and vegetable substances....

"Such is the Old Town of Manchester, and on re-reading my description, I am forced to admit that instead of being exaggerated, it is far from black enough to convey a true impression of the filth, ruin, ventilation, and health which characterise the construction of this single district, containing at least twenty to thirty thousand inhabitants. And such a district exists in the heart of the second city of England, the first manufacturing city of the world. If any one wishes to see in how little space a human being can move, how little air - and *such* air! - he can breathe, how little of civilisation he may share and yet live, it is only necessary to travel hither. True, this is the *Old* Town, and the people of Manchester emphasise the fact whenever anyone mentions to them the frightful condition of this Hell upon Earth; but what does that prove? Everything which here arouses horror and indignation is of recent origin, belongs to the *industrial epoch.* "

After expressing his horror at the appalling state of the habitations in which the masses of poor have been forced to suffer out their short lives he at last begins to lay blame where it belongs in the next few paragraphs of his vivid account.

"The couple of hundred houses, which belong to old Manchester, have been long since abandoned by their original inhabitants; the industrial epoch alone has crammed into them the swarms of workers whom they now shelter; the industrial epoch alone has built up every spot between these old houses to win a covering for the masses whom it has conjured hither from the agricultural districts and from Ireland; the industrial epoch alone enables the owners of these cattle sheds to rent them for high prices to human beings, to plunder the poverty of the workers, to undermine the health of thousands, in order that they *alone*, the owners, may grow rich. In the industrial epoch alone has it become possible that the worker scarcely freed from feudal servitude could be used as mere material, a mere chattel; that he must let himself be crowded into a dwelling too bad for every other, which he for his hard-earned wages buys the right to let go utterly to ruin. This manufacture has achieved, which, without these workers, this poverty, this slavery could not have lived. True, the original construction of this quarter was bad, little good could have been made out of it; but, have the landowners, has the municipality done anything to improve it when rebuilding? On the contrary, wherever a nook or corner was free, a house has been run up; where a superfluous passage remained, it has been built up; the value of land rose with the blossoming out of manufacture, and the more it rose, the more madly was the work of building up carried on, without reference to the health or comfort of the inhabitants, with sole reference to the highest possible profit on the principle that no hole is so bad but that some poor creature must take it who can pay for nothing better. However, it is the Old Town, and with this reflection the bourgeoisie is comforted. "

From: Friedrich Engels, <u>The Condition of the Working-Class in England in 1844</u> (London: Swan Sonnenschein & Co., 1892)

Engels' book about the English working classes contains original and influential thoughts on socialism and its development. These extracts were about the most deprived industrial cancer in Britain at the time. Although received as an intriguing revelation in Germany, in England at first it made little impact principally because it was not translated until the end of the century.

Lenin praised it with: "And, in fact, neither before 1845 nor after has there appeared so striking and truthful a picture of the misery of the working class."

The Gas Works near Angel Meadow played a central role in improving the lighting and cooking in Manchester.

ENGELS AND MARY BURNS

It should be borne in mind when thinking Engels accounts of the conditions of the working poor in Manchester that he had a very intelligent and acute albeit humble mentor in the shape and person of an Irishwoman, Mary Burns. Mary, born in 1822, was a surviving daughter of textile dyer and factory operative, Michael Burns, and Mary Conroy, Irish immigrants from Tipperary, may have begun her working life at about 9 years of age scavenging scraps of fluff off the mill machinery and the factory floor. She and he might well have met in the Owenite Hall of Science on Deansgate which   Engels visited .She was 20 years old when they met and she was no doubt physically attractive and mentally alert when Engels took up with her and they lived together as man and wife and as political colleagues and comrades for the next 20 years. Regrettably she died suddenly of a heart attack on 7 January in 1863 at the all too tender age of 40 in 252 Hyde Road, Ardwick. Her age at death was nevertheless greater than the average life expectancy of a labourer in Manchester which in 1842 was 17 years only.

Engels then took up Mary's sister Lizzy as lover/ housekeeper marrying her only when she was about to die. Marx's son-in-law remarked that Lizzy was "in continual touch with the many Irishmen in Manchester and always well informed of their conspiracies."

Apparently they both were opposed the institution of marriage regarding it as form of class oppression. The fact was Marx and Engels both frequently discussed marriage at length. In this respect a work by Richard Weikart called <u>Marx, Engels, and the Abolition of the Family</u> is revelatory.

Nevertheless Engels strongly believed in lasting monogamy because it was supportive of women. As a matter of fact many a monogamous pairing of man and woman

prevailed in Angel Meadow simply because few of the very poor could afford marriage licences or church fees. Church theologians would have called their marriages natural law marriages and therefore morally binding on both parties.

The young Friedrich Engels.

Mary's contribution to nascent socialism must have been considerable and she must have been principal among the influences mentioned by Lenin in his observation, "In Manchester he established contacts with people active in the English labour movement at the time and began to write for English socialist publications." She must have been very intelligent but lacking in formal advanced schooling. Marx's daughter Eleanor as pretty, witty and charming.

Mary Burns would have escorted Engels through the slums of Manchester and Salford helping him in his research by drawing his attention to features she would have known very well. He might well have protected him from assault as she would have been an obvious gentleman among the ragged and therefore as such an obvious target. Her obvious ability to speak fluently in the Gaelic-English patois would have taken on anywhere in the district without hurt or hindrance. They subsequently lived together off and on in Manchester for 28 years during which time Engels maintained gentleman's lodgings in one part of the city whilst at the same time renting a series of rooms in workers' districts where Mary's sister Lizzie acted as housekeeper. Publicly he lived the life as a respectable businessmen keeping a set of rooms where he entertained his for business friends, became a member of the Albert Club , name after Prince Albert, a club for German businessmen Oxford Road and hunted with the Cheshire Hunt. He did his best to hide his relationship with Mary.

Among their dwellings were: a modest house, 252 Hyde Road where they called themselves Frederick and Mary Boardman: Thorncliff Grove; a large house , 52 Richmond Grove, Chorlton on Medlock; 63/65 Cecil Street (Commercial Hotel); the last dwelling was a well-appointed house in Dover Street. **After** Engels had returned to Manchester in November 1850 they lived at 70 Great Ducie Street.

Mary's father and stepmother appeared to have been neglected however for they had to seek admission to Manchester's worst workhouse, or 'Poor Law Bastille', on New Bridge Street where Michael died in 1858 and was buried at St. Patrick's Church in Miles Platting. The stepmother was still in the workhouse in 1861. Of course Mary may not have had much if any control over Engels purse and may have had no personal income to provide for them.

According to the author Mike Dash, Engels and Mary toured Ireland together in 1856. from 'Dublin to Galway... then 20 miles north and inland, on to Limerick, down the Shannon to Tarbert, Traice and Killarney, and back to Dublin. Apparently in his letters referring to this experience Engels wrote: "I had never imagined that famine could be so tangibly real. Whole villages are deserted... and '...through systematic oppression, they have come to be a completely wretched nation and now, as everyone knows, they have the job of providing England, American, Australia, etc., with whores, day labourers, maquereaux, pickpockets, swindlers, beggars and other wretches'. (Here maquereaux probably meant whoremongers.)

Mary may well have been unlettered but like so many of the poor she would have possessed a high untutored intellect often superior to the middle and upper middle class English people who looked down upon the primitive Irish. Unfortunately little can be discovered about Mary's contributions on the political scene because Engels destroyed his letters about his personal life with Mary Burns. It is thought that she was active in the Chartist Movement, a working class political imitative strongly supported in Manchester. It is likely that she had at least an interest in the Fenian movement in Manchester.

In her time, 1867, a police van on the way through Manchester city from the courthouse was attacked by Fenians armed with revolvers, and in the attack Police Sergeant Charles Brett, seated inside the van was shot dead. Three of the thirty or so Fenians who carried out the rescue, posthumously called the Manchester martyrs, Michael O'Brien, William Philip Allen and Michael Larkin members of the Irish Republican Brotherhood were publicly hanged outside New Bailey Prison at Salford on 23 November 1867. The freed men Colonel Thomas J. Kelly and Captain Timothy Deasy were never caught. The Mancunian Irish were being very politically active in that instance.

ENGELS AND MARX

It was in 1844, while on his way back to Germany stopping over in Paris that the Engels became acquainted with Marx. Engels had by then sent a trilogy of articles to Marx and they were published in the newspapers Rheinische Zeitung and in the Deutsch–Französische Jahrbücher, describing the conditions among the working class in Manchester. The two friends jointly wrote a book entitled The Holy Family, or Critique of Critical Critique.

From 1845 to 1847 Engels returned to take up his life in Europe living in Brussels and Paris, organising the German workers and working with communists. Thus arose the famous Manifesto of the Communist Party of Marx and Engels, published in 1848. The revolution of 1848, which broke out first in France and then spread to other West-European countries, resulted in Marx and Engels returning to their native country. Friedrich Engels (1820-1895) a German philosopher, social scientist, journalist and businessman together with Karl Marx founded Marxist theory and political communism followed upon that.

Engels' high salary made it possible to support Marx financially enabling him to continue writing his major work Das Kapital. Engels disliked his own employment but did it for the good of their cause to maintain himself and Mary to some extent although she had turned down his offer of freeing her from wage dependency, and his friend Marx. Engels later collaborated with Karl Marx at Chetham's Library in the city, which famously resulted in the writing of the Communist Manifesto.

THE DAUGHTERS OF CHARITY
AND
THE BROTHERHOOD OF ST. VINCENT DE PAUL IN MANCHESTER

Interestingly although both men were highly critical of the church, while they were fully engaged in theorising about helping the poor by changing political systems, various religious charities were busily providing food, clothing and shelter directly to the poor of Manchester. Redressing situations which caused poverty was one route and relieving poverty by providing aid was yet another and more immediate route. The Ragged Schools were a case in point as was the work of the religious order of the Company of the Daughters of Charity of St Vincent de Paul. The Daughters' mission in the UK began in 1847 with a *maison de charité* right there in the City of Salford, Manchester. Unfortunately after less than two years, the Manchester house was closed by the Paris superiors in response to an arson attack and physical assaults on the sisters, motivated by anti-Catholic and anti-convent aggression. The poor had to wait a few years more for help from that quarter.

However from the time of their formation in 1844, the Daughters fraternal allies, the part time volunteers of the Brotherhood of St. Vincent de Paul were actively engaged in providing direct aid to the poor when visiting their homes in major cities in England. The poor of Manchester had to wait until after 1844 for the direct aid which their brother lay organisation The Brotherhood of St Vincent of Paul (Now known as the Society of St. Vincent de Paul of England and Wales). The Brotherhood of St Vincent de Paul founded in Paris in 1833 by a group of Catholic students who, led by Frédéric Ozanam, aimed to put their faith into action through direct contact and assistance to the poor. The English initiative began in London in 1844 having Sir Stuart Knill, Bart, Lord Mayor of London, as one of its founder members.

Astonishingly at a time when the poverty of Irish Catholics in Manchester with at an all-time low in 1845 the London head office of the Society received a letter from the President of the Manchester conference dated 9 November in which he '...mentioned that one of the clergy of the Manchester mission had requested him not to allow any of the brothers to visit the poor, or exercise any of the works of the brotherhood within his district, and also full advice upon the subject'. It is to be hoped that few of his fellow clergy followed his seriously begrudging attitude. (Reported in a re print, 1994, of Brotherhood of St. Vincent of Paul Minute Book 1844)

The members of the society complied with his request although strictly speaking the clergy had no legal jurisdiction over the Brotherhood in their work with the poor. One wonders how any clergyman could prevent the poor of this parish from benefiting from the practical help that the Brotherhood of St Vincent of Paul was dispensing especially as that help arrived on personal visits to the homes of the needy in the shape of food parcels, help with rent, help for families of prisoners, funerals, cleansing of houses and tenements, providing employment opportunities, evening classes, breakfasts and so much more such as penny banks. The society's rule book put it thus: 'No work of charity is foreign to the Society. It includes, by person-to-person contact, any form of help that relieves suffering and promotes human dignity and integrity." In 1845 the Brotherhood was actively helping the poor in Manchester out of its limited resources gained through the voluntary subscriptions of churchgoers. It often amounted to the poor helping the poor.

Fortunately the people of Angel Meadow could undergo some medical attention at the Ardwick and Ancoats Dispensary founded in 1828 in the care of its the first physician James Kay, whose <u>Moral and Physical Condition of the Working Classes (1832)</u> was based on his experiences there. Compassionate though he was, Kay was one of many who held the opinion that charity promoted rather than assisted the relief of poverty. The notion is still current today. The suggestion is that recipients will content themselves with assistance making no attempts to help themselves through employment and diligent work. A succession of papal social justice encyclicals has repeated time and again that injustice caused poverty. It does.

LENIN PRAISES ENGELS

Engels' Mancunian experiences had a big formative influence upon his work for the reformation of society. In 1895 Vladimir Ilyich Lenin wrote: "After his friend Karl Marx, Engels was the finest scholar and teacher of the modern proletariat in the whole civilised world.... In their scientific works, Marx and Engels were the first to explain that socialism is not the invention of dreamers, but the final aim and necessary result of the development of the productive forces in modern society."

Lenin attributed Engels with being the first to say that "the proletariat is not only a suffering class; that it is, in fact, the disgraceful economic condition of the proletariat that drives it irresistibly forward and compels it to fight for its ultimate emancipation. And the fighting proletariat will help itself." Engels must, nevertheless, have wondered how people such as the inhabitants of Angel Meadow could have helped themselves!

THE IRISH POOR ARE BLAMED FOR THEIR CONDITION

Historically and universally the poor are frequently blamed for their conditions, even when they are living in hovels paying extortionate levels of rent and working fourteen hours or more a day in hazardous conditions. The poor were regarded as an underclass, whose degradation was largely their own fault; frequently it was stated that God wished them to be poor; they were a semi-class of probable criminal tendencies.

Victorians just like people today distinguish between the "deserving" and the "undeserving" poor. Widows, orphans, old people and those whose sickness rendered them incapable of work were regarded as deserving and could receive help through the system of Poor Houses, degrading though these were. The other poor or unemployed were regarded as undeserving and, without any social support system in place, were left entirely to their own devices.

William Hogarth's drawing of eighteenth century Gin Lane, London is universally appropriate comment upon the life of the abject suffering poor in all major British cities and certainly Angel Meadow during the nineteenth century. Life expectancy in the Angel Meadow district was 28 years at best.

"Acquired wealth, on the other hand, was commonly seen as a visible sign of virtue: the poor were bad, the rich were good - it was a natural order. Another popular concept was that if one worked hard, this would be rewarded by an increase in wealth" Victorian Manchester. (From Life in Manchester in the 19th Century http://www.manchester2002-uk.com/history/victorian/Victorian1.html)

Jerome Caminada, the Manchester detective, with his considerable experience of crime and criminals was kinder: "I desire to say that in the treatment of our criminals I should like to see a more uniform mode of sentencing adopted. I have often stood by when men have been sentenced to terms of penal servitude which have filled me with sorrow because I have been convinced that in many cases the sentences meant either a criminal death or insanity; for, astounding as a statement may appear I have never yet known a man or a woman return from long term of penal servitude in their rational mind; and yet in all probability it is a criminal had never in the course of his or her life a single chance of getting out of the circumstances in which he or she was born, breathing through poverty an air of temptation." **(25 Years of Detective Life – a fascinating account of crime in Victorian Manchester')**

Even Engels himself attributed fault to the people of Angel Meadow when he wrote of the Irish, one of whom was actually his lover and to some extent, mentor, "These people having grown up almost without civilisation, accustomed from youth to every sort of privation, rough, intemperate, and improvident, bring all their brutal habits with them among a class of the English population which has, in truth, little inducement to cultivate education and morality." Engels uses Thomas Carlyle to back his observations and while acknowledging the latter's exaggeration with "… If we except his exaggerated and one-sided condemnation of the Irish national character, Carlyle is perfectly right."

Neither writer attributes the poverty and the alleged low moral responsibility to centuries of occupation and enslavement under English rule. Carlyle wrote "The wild Milesian features, looking false ingenuity, restlessness, unreason, misery, and mockery, salute you on all highways and byways." Yet in those Milesian times the Irish were scrupulously clean using soap in their ablutions and regularly wearing perfume.

Lisa Connell in her work: The Ultimate Scapegoat: A Study of the Irish in England During the Early Nineteenth Century, wrote "I consulted many sources, Friedrich

Engels, Leon Faucher, James Kay-Shuttleworth to name but a few and the reoccurring theme as pertaining to the Irish in all these works was mainly consistent; the Irish were a lazy, vulgar people prone to drinking and brawling." She continues, "The irony of Engels, a champion of the working class, being unable to sympathize with the Irish, the most downtrodden group, is illuminating to us, the modern day reader. If even Engels, liberal thinker that he was, subscribed to the belief of the Irish as a people who chose to live in deprivation, it becomes apparent that this belief was the norm, not the exception. Add to this Engels' involvement with an Irish servant girl, spanning twenty years and the irony becomes even greater."

As for the physical appearance of the Irish before their lands were stolen and occupied by the English invaders, an interesting observation was made by a Spanish nobleman, Don Francisco de Cuellar, a survivor from a ship wrecked along the coast of Ireland in 1588. He said, "The men are large bodied, of handsome features and limbs, and as active as the roe deer. They do not eat oftener than once a day and this is at night; and that which they usually eat is butter with oaten bread." The potato was certainly not native to Ireland but a result of an imposition of a monocultural crop upon the Irish poor while even during the Great Famine its oats, barley, wheat, milk, butter and eggs were being exported to England by the land owners.

Furthermore-in the matter of illiteracy and ignorance, in 1835 British poor will still 35 years away from the "readin', writin' and 'rithmetic" skills brought in by the Elementary Education Act of 1870 whereas in Ireland, the first of its colonies, the British government had already set up a National Education system in 1831. Poverty stricken Irish immigrants were more likely to be better schooled than their British born counterparts. In fact the informal and often secret Irish 'hedge schools' were well ahead in the medium of English let alone Gaelic.

For example, a Fernández-Suárez quotes a Board of Education inspector visiting a school in Ireland in 1835. He was: "Amazed at the skill of the twelve-year-old boys in reading the new books, and considering the possibility that they were reciting from memory, I invited one of their number to read me a passage from the gospel of Saint Matthew. Evidently the child misunderstood me. He searched in his satchel until he found his tattered book, stood up, and proceeded to read me the account of Christ's passion—in Greek (From: Local Ireland & Others 1999).

The poor, Irish or British, were, as they still are figures of fun in newspapers and broadsheets. Cartoonists and writers joined in the process of blaming the poor for their ignorance, illnesses and quarrelsomeness back then just as they do now.

In this picture the artist depicts the Irishmen in the graphic habit of the time with Simian like features.
(Irish Apes: Tactics of De-Humanization Lisa Wade, PhD)

Another drawing shown here called Contrasted Faces is a prime example of a deliberate attempt to contrast a revered Englishwoman with a reviled Irishwoman. I have no doubt Mary Burns would have looked like this Florence Nightingale rather than the Bridget McBruiser. Engels' friend was a fine looking woman whose looks drew him to her on first encounter.

CONTRASTED FACES.

" Look on this picture, and then on that."—SHAKSPEARE.

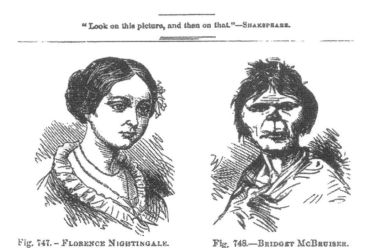

Fig. 747. – FLORENCE NIGHTINGALE.   Fig. 748.—BRIDGET MCBRUISER.

1847-48   THE MASS ARRIVAL OF IMMIGRANTS

The migrant Irish whom Engels got to know so well certainly were popularly perceived as being feckless, lacking in skills, involved in crime, heavy drinkers, living in squalor and lowering the wages of British people and generally contaminating the English people with whom they came into contact. The truth of the matter was that although many Irish preferred living in cities and engaging in industrial work rather than in the countryside they were also to be found throughout countryside towns and villages within which they integrated well with the English-born poor and were not to be distinguished from them. In the mid-19th century Lancashire became home to the greatest number of Irish migrants per head of population of all the counties in England. The biggest influx was to be found in Liverpool and the Manchester Salford conurbations. In Manchester the Irish settled predominantly in Ancoats, New Town (Irish Town), Little Ireland. Their very numbers overwhelmed the ability of local authorities to house them so they were forced to exist in very inferior accommodation in the most unsanitary conditions. Remarkably just 170 years afterwards, during Prime Minister's Question time on Wednesday 7 September 2016, the Labour Party Leader addressed the Prime Minister, "Only a year ago the Prime Minister voted against a Labour amendment to the Housing Bill which quite simply said 'all homes for rent in the private rented sector should be fit for human habitation'."

Many had fled death from starvation during and after the Great Irish Famine which lasted from 1847 to 1848. In sheer desperation many survivors fled abroad so that, for example, in the year 1847 some 300,000 Irish disembarked in Clarence Dock, Liverpool on their way to anywhere they could reach. John Hynes would then have been eight years old and Bridget Tierney, seven, and they may have entered England with their parents at that time. Certainly, 24 years later the Census recorded them as living in 25 Hargreaves Street, Ancoats, Manchester. Ancoats, with its 40% Irish population, was probably the poorest and most deprived area of the city, if not the nation. Other migrant workers settled nearby. For example, a small area of nearby Chorlton on Medlock became known as "Little Italy" on account of the large numbers of immigrant Italians who lived there in a separate ghetto-like district.

A 1901 street plan shows the Ancoats district with Hargreaves Street on the north east edge to the north on the other side of the railway lines. Near here two ragged schools, the Charter Street and the Sharp Street, took care of several hundred children each week despite the fact that when Sharp Street School began there ,in mid-century, older children threw stones through the windows, left dead cats on doorsteps and attacked the teachers as they walked to work for them in the buildings.

The Ragged University site http://www.raggeduniversity.co.uk provides snippets from the Annual Reports of the Charter Street Ragged School> Here are some of them.

1862 – School more established and becoming known in the neighbourhood. School building "meeting house of thieves and prostitutes" The school bought the building this year for £200. Soup kitchen opened with help from Cotton Famine Relief Committee (cotton famine caused by over- production, and disruption of import of baled cotton by American Civil war), the teachers at the school also worked with St Michael's committee. 20 beer houses closed in the area with help from the school. The Old Victory now a boys' hostel/night refuge. Number of thieves diminished. School helped a17 year old girl leave prostitution and saved her 12 year old sister from the same fate.

1865 – Describes filthy narrow dangerous streets and overcrowded alleys and courts, damp cellars and rickety stairs leading to obscure garrets. Beds of orange boxes and straw with 3 families sleeping in 1 room.

THE SMELLS.

The railway viaduct from Victoria Station crossed Angel Meadow where the foul air was filled with noxious smells from the polluted rivers Irk and Irwell, the Gould Street gas works, the tanneries, the piggeries and the human and animal excrement.

"The mixture was ladled further by aromas from the tannery, the dye works, the iron foundry, the brewery, the tripe works and rotting vegetation from the Smithfield market, all added together with the neighbourhood's fried fish and bad sanitation smells, one would agree that the cauldron of Angel Meadow was indeed a potent brew. "

—James Stanhope-Brown, *Angels from the Meadow*

This cartoon from PUNCH very effectively illustrates the stench of many an English city

THE ENGLISH CATHOLIC HIERARCHY AND THE POVERTY STRICKEN

The Roman Catholic hierarchy took very particular interest in the spiritual and corporal welfare of these thousands of incoming Irish because in fact this mass immigration corresponded with the passing of the Roman Catholic Relief Act of 1829 repealing the Test Act of 1672 and the various Penal Laws which had been in force for many years. In fact, for all the demonising of the Irish poor as ignorant beasts of burden, it took an Irishman Daniel O'Connell to bring about that emancipation through the British parliament.

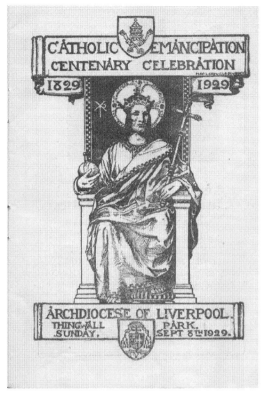

This order of service booklet issued by the Diocese of Liverpool commemorates the Centenary of Catholic Emancipation in 1929 the year in which the Bridget Hynes wife of George Hynes died in Liverpool.

Twenty one years after Emancipation the restoration of the Catholic hierarchy in England and Wales took place when Cardinal Wiseman was installed as Archbishop of Westminster in St George's Cathedral, Southwark, in December 1850.

Cardinal Wiseman, failing to live up to the historical implications of his surname, blundered, offending the establishment by proclaiming that he would now govern and 'shall continue to govern, the counties of Middlesex, Hereford, and Essex as ordinary thereof, and those of Surrey Sussex, Kent, Berks R Hampshire, with the islands and next, as admin with ordinary jurisdiction'. He meant of course that he would be governing Catholics spiritually therein but critics took the opportunity to exercise their ant-Catholicism. The newspaper The Times opportunistically commented by referring to Wiseman as "the newfangled Archbishop of Westminster" and Queen Victoria was alleged to have responded with "I am Queen of England, or am I not?"

Wiseman having been made only too aware of is very indiscreet comment responded by saying that the focus of the Catholic mission would not be political but social and it would take place in "labyrinths of lanes and courts, and alleys and slums, nests of ignorant, vice, depravity, and crime, as well as of squalor, wretchedness and disease; whose atmosphere is typhus, whose ventilation is cholera; in which swarms a huge and almost countless population, in great measure, nominally at least, Catholic; haunts of filth which no sewage committee can reach, dark corners which no lighting board can brighten". These words in fact reflected Engels own writings and the pages of Dicken's social commentaries.

Among those Catholics then in the spiritual care of the hierarchy within Angel

Meadow was a young woman, Bridget Tierney, whose father John Tierney, a migrant labourer, had taken good care of her while both living in Manchester when she was married at age 21 to a Patrick Connolly (Spelled CONLEY on the marriage entry) on 22 May, 1859 in the Catholic Parish Church. The groom, a tailor, was 20 years of age and his father was also an Irish labourer. Both bride and groom signed with marks so they must have been illiterate. When married they were both living at the same address, 62 Addington Street, Manchester. (The street is still there but only a warehouse of that century stands near that number.) A Martin Burke and an Ellen Mooney were witnesses. I now follow some of her life there through the medium of some surviving family correspondence.

THE MIGRANTS' CHILDREN ARE BORN IN THE "...OVERCROWDED HELL HOLE."

1862, July, BRIDGET CONNOLLY'S FIRST BORN

On the sixth of July, 1862, Bridget gave birth to a girl, Mary. The father was described on the birth certificate as a journeyman tailor although on Mary's later death certificate he was described as an assistant in the iron works. The birth took place where they were then living, number 1 Charlotte Street, in the St. George District of Manchester. Bridget must then have been about 24 years old. Her maiden surname was given as Tierney. As she could not write, she made her mark on the certificate. It is possible that Patrick Connolly died shortly afterwards leaving the widow Bridget to partner John Hynes, sometime between 1864 and 1868.

This was a year when Engels told Marx that he was living with his Mary, a Mary Burns, almost all the time to save money but was reluctant to give up his lodgings and to move in with her altogether.

1869, January GEORGE HINES (HYNES) BORN IN HARGREAVES STREET

On the twenty sixth of January, 1869, the year of Engels retirement from his employment, George Hines, was born in 25 Hargreaves Street, Red Bank in the middle of a district in which people suffered the direst poverty. His father's name was written as John Hines, his occupation was that of foundry labourer; the mother, Bridget Hines was formerly Tierney. The informant, given as 'Mother', Bridget Hines made her mark.

Registrars of all the children's births and also the census enumerators recorded the surname as Hines, obviously their preferred rendition. However, on John Hynes' death certificate of 1885 the name was written, Hynes. That same year George signed 'George Hynes' on the Army attestation. George probably used the preferred spelling of the name as used in the Catholic elementary school.

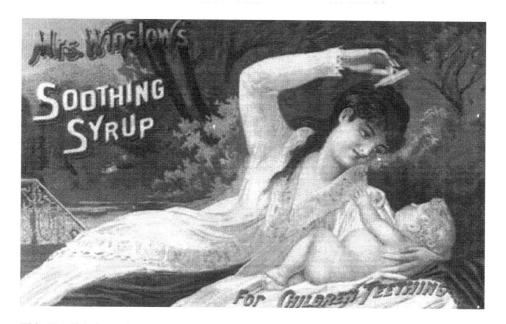

This English born boy, George, was to spend his childhood growing up in Angel Meadow among the lodging houses, drinking dens, industrial stores and "putty shops" which fenced stolen goods. There he no doubt played among pig pens aplenty and possibly stood with other children peeping into the accessible slaughter houses surrounded by discarded offal and dung. These children would run barefoot through the pools of the all too few neighbourhood privies overflowing with urine and faeces so that the house at the bottom of slopes received the excrement day and night. Pickpockets, beggars, prostitutes and hawkers (George's mother was a hawker) plied their trades. Unhygienic "tommy shops" sold penny a pint pea soup and druggists sold large quantities of baby syrups laced with laudanum which overwrought mothers fed to waling babies to shut them up. Among other brands Mrs. Winslow's Soothing Syrup, a morphine-based formula was used as a remedy for infant's "teething sickness." It was dangerous stuff.

As an alert intelligent boy he would no doubt have been able to point out all the industrial features: the foundry ironworks, the dye works, brickfields, paper mill, paint works, stone works, wheelwrights, saw mills, chemical works, starch and gum works, machine engineers, glass works, a plaster of Paris processing, locomotive engineering works, colliery, rope works, petroleum distillery and the huge gas generating works. I have no doubt they all held great fascination for him and no doubt when as a mature adult he became foreman and then manager of a mill in Liverpool.

In his book Angel Meadow: Victorian Britain's Most Savage Slum, Dean Kirby writes of the "Beer houses with names such as the Flying Ass and the Dog and Duck were dens for gangs of robbers and confidence tricksters with glorious names such as Jemmie the Crawler and Cabbage Ann. And these places, one Victorian observer wrote, were the rendezvous of the elder thieves, the fighting men, the swindlers and mutilated beggars."

1871 CENSUS

On the 1871 census return, John Hines' birthplace is given as Manchester whilst Bridget's was given as Ireland. He was 32 and she 33, while her daughter Mary was given as 9 years old also born in Manchester. George, my grandfather, was just two. As a result of the passing of the Elementary Education Act 1870 the lives of the children of Angel Meadow and indeed of the whole nation were to be vastly improved through their compulsory attendance at school.

1871, August, ELLEN HINES BORN

Later in the year, on the second of August, Ellen Hines, a younger sister for George, was also born in 25 Hargreaves Street. She was grandmother of my cousin Ellen McCormick, living in Canada who holds the family correspondence cited here.

1873, November, MARGARET HINES BORN

On the second of November, 1873, Margaret was also born in Hargreaves Street. The birth was registered by a Mary Kelly, listed as 'Occupier' of 25 Hargreaves Street. That simple entry says a lot about the overcrowding suffered among the poor of that neighbourhood at that time. Perhaps they consumed their shares of soothing syrups and other quack remedies which prevailed at the time.

1877 June JOHN THOMAS HYNES BORN

On the twentieth of June 1877, as reported by Martha Williams of 25 Brown Street, Red Bank, Manchester, John Thomas Hines was born to John Hines and Bridget Hines formerly Connolly living in 25 Hargreaves Street.

At the time Hargreaves Street comprised multi occupancy houses once homes of the better off Mancunians but by then let to poor incomers. Today the street, situated on the northern side of the River Irk contains one or two shops but the grounds on either side street are car parks festooned with litter.

From Hargreaves Street access to Angel Meadow was gained by walking under the gloomy railway viaduct slung across the Irk Valley. By then Angel Meadow had long been transformed from a pleasant suburb to a sordid, overcrowded slum. The air was permanently polluted by obnoxious smells from the Irk and Irwell and the Gould Street gas works.

According to the Fleet Street journalist Angus Bethune Reach the district was in its day ' The lowest, most filthy, most unhealthy, and most wicked locality in Manchester… inhabited by prostitutes, their bullies, thieves, cadgers, vagrants, tramps, and, in the very worst sties of filth and darkness, by those unhappy wretches the low Irish.' (Morning Chronicle, 12 November 1849 cited in Angel Meadow by Dean Kirby.)

Gustav Dore's engraving: Over London, in the late 19 century is as good an example of the Irk Street viaduct and housing as one could ever have found.

1881 THE FAMILY NOW LIVING IN IRK STREET

By that year the family had moved their few belongings and themselves deeper into Angel Meadow and into inferior accommodation in Irk Street in the dark shadow of the railway embankment amid its noise and noxious odours.

In his book Journeys to England and Ireland, Alexis de Tocqueville was describing the Irk Street district when he wrote:

"On ground below the level of the river and overshadowed on every side by immense workshops, stretches marshy land which widely spaced muddy ditches can neither drain nor cleanse. Narrow, twisting roads lead down to it. They are lined with one-story houses whose ill-fitting planks and broken windows show them up, even from a distance, as the last refuge a man might find between poverty and death. None-the-less the wretched people reduced to living in them can still inspire jealousy of their fellow human beings. Below some of their miserable dwellings is a row of cellars to which a sunken corridor leads. Twelve to fifteen human beings are crowded pell-mell into each of these damp, repulsive holes."

In 1844, the Oldham Road terminus of the Manchester–Leeds Railway was abandoned and the line extended through Collyhurst to a new link station at Hunts

Bank – the first Victoria Station. A railway viaduct traversed Angel Meadow, whilst the obnoxious smells from the Irk and Irwell and the Gould street gas works darkened the landscape.

A doctor's visit to Irk Street in 1844 is recorded in Friends of Angel Meadow:

"Anne Hannah, aged 8 - No. 23, Back Irk Street. E. Father a weaver. C. A very fine girl. N.S not subject to disordered bowels. E.C had supped on porridge and buttermilk. L.C.F &c house furnitureless, dirty, containing six children and two adults, just opposite the house the common sewer discharges its contents which run down the street for several hundred yards into the river, gas and ammonia works a little higher up."

The 1881 census records the family, except Mary, as living in number 12 Irk Street right on the edge of the largest pauper burial ground in Manchester. This time John Hines' place of birth was given as Ireland, his age as 42 and his occupation as labourer in an iron works. Bridget was 39. [According to the returns she had then become younger than John (!) although the 1871 census makes her a year older than he!] Her occupation was given as hawker that is a street vendor, selling goods from baskets and trays. George was 12 years old, Ellen was 9, Margaret was 6, all attended school (Compulsory elementary education had begun in 1870 and ironically earlier back in Ireland!) and John T. Hynes was 3 years of age.

The Irish had to resort to and rely upon multiple- occupancy. In Angel Meadow it was most often 10 persons per house whereas in the non-Irish houses in neighbouring areas it was down to 6.4 persons per house. This was not due to frequent lack of accommodation because there were always some empty houses in the area. The reason was that the cost of the rents forced low-income people into sharing the space and the rent between two families within the same dwelling. A comment from the Manchester Guardian dated 6 February 1847 is pertinent: "...the population of the district of St Georges is, to a great extent, composed of the law of the Irish, who live in large together in great numbers in the same house. In one part of the district called Angel Meadow, it is not uncommon to find 20 or 30 persons living in one house, when there is not accommodation for one third of that number."

The Hynes family was no exception. The England and Wales Census of 1881 lists two families living at that address:

Name	Status	Gender	Age	
John Hines	Head	Male	42	Ireland
Bridget Hines	Wife	Female	39	Ireland
George Hines	Son	Male	12	Manchester
Ellen Hines	Daughter	F	9	Manchester
Margaret Hines	Daughter	F	6	Manchester
John T Hines	Son	M	3	Manchester
Mary Barrett	Lodger Head	F	40	Ireland
John Barrett	Son	M	17	Ireland
Thomas Barrett	Son	M	15	Manchester
Michael Barrett	Son	M	11	Manchester

Irk Street stretched or rather hunched itself up below the railway viaduct so it may well have been the place described by Engels when he wrote, *"Immediately under the railway bridge there stands a court filth and horrors of which surpass all the others by far, just because it was hitherto so shut off, so secluded that the way to it could not be found without a good deal of trouble."*

Mary living as a boarder nearby
The 1881 British Census reported Mary Connolly living nearby as a boarder.

Dwelling: 9 Elizabeth Ann
Census Place: Manchester, Lancashire, England
Source. FHL Film 1341954: Pro Ref RG11. Place 4000 Folio 109 Page 34

	Marr	Age	Sex	Birthplace
Ellen AUSTIN	Widow	60	F	Ireland
Re Head				
Occ: Housekeeper				
Mary AUSTIN				
Ref Daur				
Occ: Brush Maker	Unmarried	24	F	Manchester
Rosean AUSTIN				
Ref Daur				
Occ: Brush Maker	Unmarried	22	F	Ireland
Sarah HILL				
Ref Boarder				
Occ: Brush Maker	U	19	F	Manchester
Mary CONNOLLY				
Ref Boarder				
Occ: confectioner	U	19	F	Manchester

The four brush makers perhaps made their products in their own home.

These families like others of the respectable poor would have had to struggle hard to uphold their moral rectitude but uphold it they did. I draw attention to the fact that the Barrett family living in the Hynes comprised a widow and three sons, two of whom were close in age to Mary Connolly. One may suppose that for the sake of propriety her parents had arranged for her to take of lodgings in the household comprised entirely of women. Such an arrangement would go a long way towards avoiding any hints of impropriety. It is likely that such arrangements were common practice among the poor Irish Catholics to protect the modesty of marriageable age daughters.

1881, THE CONVENT OF THE GOOD SHEPHERD

By the time Mary had reached her nineteenth birthday, a place destined to play a significant part in her short life had been well established in Fulham Road, London, the Convent of the Good Shepherd where Mary became a religious sister. The Convent belonged to the Institute of the Good Shepherd, which was a branch of 'Our Lady of Charity of the Refuge,' founded in France in 1641.

The order Our Lady of Charity of the Refuge was started in seventeenth century France by Father John Eudes and his initiative was followed up by Mary Euphrasia Pelletier, born on 31 July 1796 who joined the order in 1816 but went on to found an offshoot called the Congregation of Our Lady of Charity of the Good Shepherd providing compassionate care and healing for young women and the marginalized within their society and communities. Those cared for did not have to be Catholics.

Mary Euphrasia Pelletier

One source, Le Brun, C. (1909) transcribing for New Advent by Joseph P. Thomas rather explicitly wrote "The aim of this institute is to provide a shelter for girls and women of dissolute habits, who wish to do penance for their iniquities and to lead a truly Christian life. 'Dissolute' was certainly another way of describing those unfortunate women! These women who were rescued and protected by the sisters were called penitents and also magdalens after Mary Magdalen who as a follower of Jesus was supposedly a reformed prostitute according to Pope Gregory the Great. Modern scholars have decided that she was no such thing. She was instead a respectable disciple.

The sisters in this religious order practised an austere, contemplative life with prayer, penance and manual labour as its principal occupations. After taking the usual vows of poverty, chastity and obedience these sisters took a fourth vow and that was to work for the protection, conversion and instruction of 'penitents.' The Penitents who agreed to remain became 'magdalens.' The resident rescued girl children living in the convents were called 'Preservates'. All cared-for residents were taught self-respect and industrious habits.

The girls and women were accommodated in strictly segregated and architecturally separated parts of the convents. There were individual buildings for penitent women, for the Order of Magdalene, for girls between the ages of seven and eighteen and for the nuns themselves.

Some of the Sisters had arrived in England from their Mother Homes in Angers, France in May 1841 and opened a convent and Home for Women in Hammersmith, London.

Mary Connolly

Sister Mary of St. Bertha

1881, May MARY CONNOLLY ENTERS A RELIGIOUS ORDER

Mary entered the novitiate of the Good Shepherd in May 1881. In taking up a vocation in a religious order devoted to the domiciliary care of the most marginalized and abused women of the nation, Mary was one of the many who despite the dreadful living conditions and the low expectations of men like Kay and Engels, their friends, aspired to the good moral life and the service of others.

Engels and Kay and others were looking at the lives and practices of these people of Angel Meadow from the top down. They were the ones who wielded power and influence based upon education and monetary privilege but using this opportunity we can look at the social history from the bottom up from the perspectives of the powerless and underprivileged. The inhabitants of Angel Meadow had their own ways of coping and avoiding the criminality of some of their neighbours. All communities had their informal experts. They had their mid-wives, their God siblings expert in delivering babies and supporting the mothers. They had their healers with the traditional herbs and spices. They had the women who were good at laying out the dead to give them as decent a burial as could be afforded. They even had, God help them, their back street abortionists. They no doubt had ways of sorting out men who physically assaulted their wives. The woman's brothers probably lived nearby and could be called upon to punch the daylights out of the offender. It has been known for tough priests to undertake the task! They had their letter writers who would take dictation or a few pence. The poor of Angel Meadow could not afford to pay professionals, nor pay stipend to clergy to conduct marriages and requiems for the souls of the departed. Alexis de Tocqueville thought Manchester to be anarchic and lacking in municipal orderliness and he was right. There were really no social services and there were no even sewers to take away the human waste products, the offal and the pig manure.

The first of these preserved family letters sent to Bridget was from her daughter Mary and written by her because by then she had learned her skills at school thanks to the Elementary School Act of 1870. It was undated, but was probably written sometime between April 1881 and December 1881, in the Convent of the Good Shepherd, Hammersmith, London. It would have to be later than the census of 1881 because then Mary was lodging with Mrs. Austin and her daughters, Rosean and Mary. In this letter, Mary tells her mother that she has been received for her *"clothing"* a stage in entering the novitiate. She ends the letter with her signature Mary Connolly. This is the only time that Mary signs her full name in this way. Subsequent letters are signed with her religious name. Mary entered the novitiate of the good Shepherd in May, 1881.

I have kept the original spellings of the letters throughout as they are personal characteristics of the writers which had I feel have to be retained. All letters were of course handwritten but they have been presented here in typescript.

CORRESPONDENCE AMONG THE MEMBERS OF AN ANGEL MEADOW FAMILY

FIRST LETTER FROM MARY TO HER PARENTS

Convent of the Good Shepherd, Hammersmith, London W

Live Jesus and Mary

Dear Mother and father
I am sure you will be very pleased to hear that I have been received for my Clothing and it will take place on the twenty fifth of this month there is one sister getting professed and four with my self receiving the Holy Habit so I will not be alone I will I will be going in a retreat on the twenty second so I want Elizze to rember me to sister Isabella and ask her if she would say the office for me and also to ask Maggie Donnelly and the McCormicks if they would go to holy Communion for me I know you will go yourself. I felt very gratfull to my little brother for the nice picture he sent me so I am giving this one to Nelly and she must ask George to learn her the prayer that is on the back and she must say it every day. I was very sorry to hear of Maggie McGee coming home but the Will of God must be done.

I remain Dear Mother & father, Your Affectionate Child, Mary Connolly.
In union with the sacred Heart of Jesus & Mary
I very humbly recommend myself to all your prayers

Sister Isabella was probably a religious sister working in the family home parish in Manchester. Mary mentioned two women who were regular communicants. She has received a picture from her little brother John and she is asking her brother George to teach a prayer to her sister Ellen. The family are obviously doing their best to be good Catholics and she expects that of them.

1882 SECOND LETTER FROM MARY, probably early 1882

From our Convent of GP in Hammersmith, London, W2
{Here there was a Convent impress stamp a kind of logo, unclear}
L.J.V.M., The Heart of Jesus gives us strength for our great struggles

My very Dear Mother and father I received your kind and welcome letters and was very sorry to hear of my Father Leg been burnt. I will pray that it may soon be better. Dear Mother I hope you were as comfortable at Christmas and New Year as I wished you. As for myself I never spent one like this for I had the happiness of receiving our Lord at midnight mass. What I never had in the world. and on Christmas Day and New Years day we went to the children and they made very nice recreation. I am very well and very happy and I do not feel the time passing away. I was very pleased to hear of Nelly been confirmed and the nice name she took for it was my name when I was a postulant. We had Exposition of the Blessed Sacrament on the Feast of the Presentation & the Feast of the Immaculate Conseption and I did pray very particularly for you Dear Mother and my little Brother and sisters and also I did remember Rosanna and Ellizze. I must tell you some thing about the Feast of Holy Innocence the Novices all had recreation and the professional sisters lent us there silver hearts and the youngest Chior Novice was our Mother for that day. And our Novice mistress gave us permission to do what we liked so you may depend I did enjoy myself Dear Elizze I was very gratfull for the nice picture you sent me and also for the new picture George and Nelly sent me Dear Elizze I hope you will remember ...Father Burke and tell him how I am going on I hope he as fullfilled is promises with St. Williams Crib. I must conclude in sending my love to Mrs. Austin and all my Dear sisters & the McCormick(s) & Maggie Donnelly and excpects the same Dear Mother and Father wishing you all the graces and blessing of the coming year In union with the S. Heart of Jesus & Mary.
Your affectionately S. M. of St. Bertha N.S.C.

She uses an Irish to English construction, 'I did pray...' and ' I did remember..' reflecting her parents' usages .Obviously the McCormicks, Donnellys and Austins are good friends and we discover that Father Burke is at their parish church of St. William. The church founded in 1864 closed in 1946.

She also mentions the Immaculate Conception, which she spells incorrectly. The term entered popular usage after the 1858 apparitions in Lourdes when Bernadette agreed with the Church authorities that her vision had announced herself a The Immaculate Conception. It is likely that devotions and prayers to the Immaculate Conception were very popular at this time when health treatment for the poor was primitive. One could always hope for a miraculous cure!

John, her father, would probably have worked in the Union Bridge Iron Works when he burned his leg

1882, April THIRD LETTER FROM MARY

Convent of the Good Shepherd, Hammersmith, London, April 20th. 1882

L. J. & M., God above

Dear Mother and Father I received your kind and welcome letter and also the letter Anne Mooney sent me I was very gratfull to her for the nice picture she sent me and I did remember her very particular in my prayers I was sorry to hear of her going to America but I hope it will be all for the best. Dear Mother I am very glad to hear that you are all well and that my Father is able to go back to work and I hope he has been to his Easter Duty during the misson. Dear Mother I hope John Thomas is able to go to school now that George has left. Just before lent we had Exposition of the Blessed Sacrament for two hours every day for eight day and then came the forty hours Exposition. And the Blessed Sacrament was exposed. All through two nights so you may be sure that I did not forget you Dear Mother and my little Brothers and sisters. I was very sorry to hear of Mrs. McCormick been so ill but I hope she is getting better for I am sure they will all be but about. Dear Elizze I did pray for your intention and I was so glad to hear that you have went back to Father Burke. Dear Elizze I hope you will remember me to S. Isabella & S. Magdalene and also to Maggie Donnelly and tell her to remember to S.Patrick & S.Gita I did nor forget S.Patrick on her Feast . Give my love to all and exped the same yourselfs.

I am in union with the S. Heart of Jesus & Mary. Your affectionate daughter S. My of S. Bertha Novice of our Lady of Charity.

Migration to America is mentioned and no doubt many a one travelled there from her neighbourhood, never to return to their families. As a pious child she may well have been in the habit of reminding her parents and siblings of their religious obligations. She was prompting her father to make his Easter Duties, that was to go to confession and communion across Eastertide. It is to be hoped that these ill-nourished Catholics of St. William's parish were excused fasting and abstinence! She mentions several religious sisters: Patrick, Gita, Isabella & Magdalene who must have lived and worked in Angel Meadow.

1882, On 25 September Mary officially became a novice in the Convent.

1883, May: MARY PROFESSED AS A RELIGIOUS SISTER

After living, praying and working for two years in the Novitiate Mary was professed on the 26 September, 1883 and received her first appointment, joining the Community in Cardiff. Here is a contemporary line about the convent: "In this manor is Ty Gwyn (otherwise Pen-y-lan Farm), now the Convent of the Good Shepherd."

I add a modern note about the former Bristol convent, now a hotel: "A mile from Bristol city centre (along the A4, Bath Road), this impressive 'false gothic' building dates from the 1760s, when it was built by a wealthy Quaker businessman. It still retains a good number of original features that give its comfortable interior a unique atmosphere. The Cloisters Restaurant, for example, is set in a converted chapel - the building was home to The Sisters of the Order of the Good Shepherd, a Roman Catholic convent for many years up until the late 1940s. Don't worry - it's rather less austere these days and is very comfortable and cosy!"

1883 FOURTH LETTER FROM MARY

Convent of the Good Shepherd, Pen –y-lan, Cardiff

(My note: Today Penylan is a district and community in the east of Cardiff, Wales, known for its Edwardian era period houses and spacious tree lined roads and avenues.)

S. J.& M.
My very dear Mother & Father
I have been expecting a letter every day since our profession and a not got one yet if I had you here I would give you good scolding for it for I don't know wether you received the letter I wrote to you after our profession. I have begun to think that perhaps it as got mislaid as you have not answered it ....nine o clock on the Monday morning and arrived in Cardiff between three and four in the afternoon-we were received most kindly and was taken in to a little room where in came S An Blessed Margaret and gave us a most hearty welcome and told me what you use to say to her Mother. Her Mother told her when she came to see her. This is a very nice place you can see nothing but green fields all around plenty of apples and black berries I am sure Georgee and Nelly would like to be here I am beginning to feel quite at home and very happy and I do not feel the time passing ...dear Mother I hope all at home is thanking our Lord for the great grace He has bestowed upon one by calling me to be a religious and particular to the Good Shepherd for how many poor souls would be lost only for this order now dear Mother I ave you to promise our Lord through the grace He as given me to see that all at home goes regular to Church for I never go to Holy Communion but what I always ask our Lord to Shower down on us blessing you all at home. The Sisters have been in a retreat for eight days before the

Feast of the Presentation and on the Feast we had Exposition of the ...Sister renewed their vows at the alter just has the Priest was holding the Host to give them Holy Communion and I had this great happiness for the first time I do wonder what heaven must be when we can have such happiness on earth I know my dear Mother I must finish for I want this letter to go quick to you and please write as soon you can and let me know if you did receive two letters I wrote to you after our professions. My fondest love to all at home and Roseann & Mary mrs.

I am in union with the sacred Heart of Jesus and mary. Your very affectionate Child

In this letter Mary chastises her parents for not writing sooner. As eloquently as she can in her simple prose Mary says how happy she is in her religious life. The contrast and the company must have been quite delightful for this young woman who grew up in that appalling district in Manchester.

FIFTH LETTER FROM MARY Undated but no doubt December

Convent of the Good Shepherd, Pen –y-lan, Cardiff
S. J.& M.
My very dear Mother & Father

I thought I would be on time this year to wish you all a very happy Christmas and all the graces and blessing our dear little Infant Lord will bestow on you all if you will only ask Him for them the more we ask the more pleasure He is with us so I want my dear little brother and sisters to pay a visit every day to the crib and...{writing obscure here}...little Infant to make them pleasing to Himself and rather let them die than displease Him. How are you all getting on you have not written lately I hope it is not because you are sick or anything the matter Perhaps it is like me nothing much to city we are very busy preparing for Christmas so I know you will excuse a short letter my dear Mother still ever in my next letter if you go out every day and if John as plenty of work and where he is living and above all if you are attending the Church I do often pray for you for I know you have a great deal to do but our Lord will help you if you will only trust in Him for being so generous in giving me to serve Him and you may be sure dear Mother that you will be in my mind on Christmas eve- when I receive our dear Infant Lord in Holy Communion I am very very happy and don't feel the time passing away we had a very nice day on the feast of the Immaculate Conception exposition of the Blessed Sacrament and eighteen made Children of Mary some of them have been trying 3 or 4 years so it is not as easy too be made children of Mary here as in the world they are as good. Their was two Sisters professed last Wednesday at Hammersmith the first profession since ours one of them went of Finchley and the other to Bristol so yu see they all get turned out after their profession I suppose it is very cold now it is never very cold here and have always got floures to decorate the alter now dear Mother I must finish and you will tell me what sort of a Christmas you have all had I hope you will not think I have been preaching to you much love to all at home pleas remember me to Rosanne and Mary I will not forget to pray for them as it is the first Christmas without a Mother and I want them to answer my questions.

In union with the sacred Heart of Jesus and Mary

Your affectionate Child
Sr. Mary of St. Bertha
Please excuse this untidy letter as I wrote it in a great hurry1885, March

Mary obviously looks forward to letters from home and misses them if they are not regularly sent. She takes every opportunity to remind her family of their religious duties. This time she is keen for them to visit the Christmas crib. She thanks her mother for her generosity in allowing her to enter religious life.

1885 LETTER FROM AN ELLEN HYNES, A COUSIN

Oldham March 15th. 1885

My Dear Cousin Maggie I take the pleasure of writing you those few lines hoping they may find you in as good health as this leaves me in the preasant thank god for his kind Mearcies to us all Amen and I am glad to say that my aunt is hear with us today Dear Cousin Ellen I hope you and Cousin Maggie and George and uncle will be hear on good Friday and I will pay your affair back Dear uncle I hope you wont desceive us this time Cousin Ellen you are as welcome as Maggie *Dear Brother John I hope you will come ecording to your promises * please Answer by return of post .No more at preasant from your loving friend Ellen Hynes Direct your letter to No. 3 wool st off Wall st Oldham

(* This may have been added by the older woman confirming she is John Hynes sister or sister-in-law!) The word affair probably should have been written 'fare' which this Ellen is promising to refund her visitors.

Ellen McCormick comments, 'This letter is from a cousin who also appears to be an Ellen Hynes but we cannot be certain of the name here due to a lack of punctuation. Nevertheless, the 1881 census shows an Ellen Hines at 11 Schoolcroft, Oldham, age 47, born in Castlebar and having a daughter, also Ellen, born 1860 but there is no evidence of any connection with our family. There is a Wall Street in Oldham to this very day but Schoolcroft has gone. Comment: Could this older Ellen have been an unmarried mother and sister of John? She writes 'brother John'. Or could the older Ellen have been the wife of a Thomas Hynes, mentioned elsewhere a possible brother of John.

1885, August DEATH OF JOHN HYNES

A death certificate recorded the death of John Hynes as the 11 August, 1885 aged 42. The cause of death was pulmonary congestion as certified by a G. Robinson; MRCS The informant was his widow who was present at this death. He succumbed to the same killer affliction as many thousands who lived that appalling toxic place called Angel Meadow.

(Comment by Ellen McCormick, Please notice that the reported age at death is the same as the age on the 1881 census five years earlier! Bridget wasn't consistent in reporting her own or John's age.)

GEORGE HYNES JOINS THE ARMY AT AGE SIXTEEN

This letter from George, dated the 24 September, 1885, was sent from Bowerham Barracks in Lancaster a month before he signed up for short service on the 24 October, 1885. He was accepted through a kind of circumventing –the- rules procedure which arranged for recruits to be billeted and drilled in Bowerham as militia (a kind of territorial army) during those few weeks before signing up for service in the regular army.

Question 13 on the short service attestation asked, "Do you now belong to, or have you ever served in, the militia…?" Those few weeks at Bowerham made it possible for him to reply, "Yes, 4th Btn Lancaster Regt." Recruits were probably told to write that to cover a training period of militia part-time service which enabled uncomplicated entry into regular service.

A private of the King's Own Regiment
circa 1886

In mid -Victorian Britain, 30% of the British regular army were Irish and many like George were English born of Irish parents. He followed the pattern. On the 24 October, 1885, George signed up with the Royal Lancaster Regiment, in Lancaster, at age 16 years and 9 months plus, passing himself off as being 18 years and two months and no doubt the recruiting sergeant agreeing with the deception. His home parish in Manchester was listed as St. Michael's and his occupation was labourer. The army was to be his home for some years and his quarters in a barrack block no doubt superior to anything he might have had in Angel Meadow. His army number was 1311. His height was 5 feet 5 and a quarter inches, his weight was 115 pounds, his chest measurement was 34 inches, his eyes were blue, his hair brown and he was listed as a Catholic. Under 'distinctive marks' it says: 'Tattoo C.H. G.H. arm indefinite outside left forearm. Blue …left thumb. Two blues dots outside right forearm.'

By joining the army at age sixteen George was able to avoid having to join in gang warfare as a Scuttler in Manchester. This was a time when the peculiar and very dangerous phenomenon called 'scuttling' was at its peak. According to Andrew Davies in his book The Gangs of Manchester, Scuttlers were boys between the ages of 14 and 19 working in gangs and fighting other gangs often by appointment with an array of weapons inflicting terrible wounds on each other ; all simply just for the sake of fighting.

MORE CORRESPONDENCE

1885, September LETTER FROM GEORGE HYNES

His first letter home was written when he was a temporary militia recruit, a month or so before signing up as a regular soldier.

Sep. 24th. 1885

Dear Mother, I recieved your kind and welcome letter and I am glad, to hear that you and my dear sisters and brothers are in good health. You can tell John Thomas in that I'll [part of letter missing]

..it as given me such an appetite that I can eat double as much as when I was at home. Dear Mother I was very sorry to hear of the row you had with Bella Smith I hope she will get six months for running down dear Fathers name who now lies in the grave [part missing] and I hope you will watch over the house. I am glad to hear that Maggie is going to school every day. I hope she has given over telling them little Storys I hope she will not get angry because it is only a joke of mine. Dear Mother I am so pleased that you have signed the pledge. And I `hope my dear brother John is keeping is school, every day so I must conclude in sending my kind love & best respects. From your ever beloved son George Hynes. Dear Sister Ellen you can show this letter to James Marshall and I ad to hear that he as got work because I was frightened he would lose the other eye and I am glad aslo of John Lyons and the little Squire. "Tommy Dillon". You must excuse for writing such a little letter as because I was in such a hury so Good bye

Private George Hynes
948 D. Company
4th. Kings Own Regt
Bowerham Barracks
Lancaster

It is obvious that his mother has reported some disparaging talk about his father. There is a hint of his sister having been truanting and lying about her absences. One wonders whether his mother's signing of the pledge was a pious precautionary measure or because she was herself addicted to drink and promising to cease. The Temperance Society did its best to persuade people to abstain from alcoholic beverages. The most active proponent within Catholicism and the Irish was Fr. Theobald Matthew and many a parish followed his example.

1885 26 November LETTER FROM THE SUPERIOR OF THE CONVENT TO BRIDGET HYNES

Whatever the time lag between a Christmas letter sent by Mary at Christmas time in either 1883 year or 1884 for which we have no correspondence she must have been taken very ill as shown in this surviving latter of November 1885.

Dear Mrs. Hynes

Our dear Sister was worse yesterday but had a good night so is brighter today. We were hoping to hear from you, so I now enclose a directed envelope in case you are puzzled about the directions tho I thought I wrote it very plain. Your dear daughter sends her love & hopes you are all well. You must go on praying for her as she does for you. I have written to Fr. Burke to ask his prayers. Believe me in the sacred Heart
 Very truly
St. Mary of the Good Shepherd Superior

1885, December LETTER FROM GEORGE TO HIS MOTHER

3 December, 1885
Dear Mother
I write you these few lines hoping you may be in good health as it leaves me at present. I recieved that likeness as John Delaney sent up and I think he was taken well and it wont be long before I write one to him And I think it was a nice letter he sent me. Dear Mother I don't know whether we are going to Aldershot before Christmas or not but if we are not I will try and get a few days pass I have sent a little present of a cushion which was made by a soldier with my name on it. I suppose you will not [George left out the word ' know'] what this will mean. A.P.G.H. 4 Bt A present from George Hynes 4th. Kings own which you will receive to Morrow Afternoon by a pal of mine that his going on pass. So I hope you will write soon and tell me when you received it. So I have no more to say at present. So I must conclude in sending my kind love and best respects to you all and also to John Delaney. And I am glad to hear that Nelly is still at her work and that Maggie is going to school every day and it wont be long before I see john Thomas again. So no more at present from Your Beloved son George Hynes

His Army Record states that he served in the regimental depot between the 24 October, 1885 and the 16 December 1885, so he must have written the above letter there while he was still in basic training.

'Likeness' was no doubt the Mancunian Irish local usage for photograph. Here George mentions a cushion embroidered by a fellow soldier with "A.P.G.H. 4 Bt. A present from George Hynes 4th. Kings Own'. Presumably the A.P.G.H is an abbreviation for Acting Private George Hynes. It is intriguing to know that a young soldier comrade must have been taught embroidery and practised it unselfconsciously. Did he also make the cushion one wonders?

1885, December

George was posted to the 1st. Battalion on the 17 December, 1885. While serving there he gained his 4th Class Certificate of Education. One may suppose, from what was written in a letter from the sister St. Mary, the posting must have been to Aldershot.

In the matter of army certificates of education Prussia, a militant nation was first in the field. Tax-funded compulsory primary elementary schooling was introduced in Prussia under Frederick the Great principally to improve the skills of a fighting army. In Britain army certificates of education were introduced in 1861 and linked with suitability for promotion.

The 4th Class Certificate of Education was attained for showing a very basic level of skills. At first the third-class certificate of education was considered to be set at too high given the low levels of literacy of many army recruits hence the introduction of a very basic 4th and in fact it was abolished in 1888.

George would not have needed any special instruction to gain that certificate. He did however go on to gain his 3rd and his 2nd and possibly his 1st but we have no record of the latter and that was reserved for people seeking commissioning from the ranks.

A candidate for the 3rd class certificate had to read aloud and to write down dictated passages from easy narrative and he had to work examples in the four compound rules of arithmetic and the reduction of money. Possession of a 3rd class certificate was needed for promotion to the rank of corporal. Attainment of a 2nd class certificate was necessary for promotion to sergeant so the candidate had to write and dictate from more difficult work. He had to show familiarity with all forms of regimental accounting and with arithmetical proportions, interest, fractions and averages.

First-class certificates were necessary for commissions from the ranks. Candidates had to read and take dictation from any standard author; make a fair copy of a manuscript; demonstrate their familiarity with more complicated mathematics, except cube and square root and stocks and discount; and as well prepare for examination in at least one of a number of additional subjects.

1885 LETTER FROM SISTER MARY OF THE GOOD SHEPHERD

15 Dec 85 Bristol
All for the glory of God
Dear Mrs. Hynes
I hope you have understood my silence to mean that yr dear child S.M S Bertha is going on much the same & we cannot tell the least how it will end. We had great hopes about a week ago that the internal abscess would dry up, but it continues discharging Yesterday we feared it was worse but the Doctor did not think so, tho she had a bad night she said she felt better in herself this morning. We must leave all in the hands of our good god to whom she has given herself He will ordain what is best for her. Our dear sister was much pleased with her Sister's letter & I am going to write to her brother.

Hoping you are better. I remain in the Sacred Heart

Very Truly Sr Mary of the Good Shepherd

The Bristol property, Arnos Court, had been bought for the sisters by William Austin Gillow, born 1826, into an old Lancashire furniture making Catholic family, who had been so impressed by Hammersmith Cumberland and the caring being done for women caught up in life on the streets enabled the sisters to carry out similar work in Bristol. The Cumberland was dedicated by Bishop Clifford in March 1859 and among the gifts donated by the Bishop was a chalice given him by Pope Pius IX. He also gifted land which became the Cemetery of the Holy Souls.

The first home on site there housed older teenagers and women aged between 17 to 40 years who had personal problems. At this time when child offenders as young as nine were being sent to prison performing punitive hard labour the Catholic hierarchy received permission from the Home Office to set up a reformatory school at Arnos Court. St Joseph's school, was thus set up in April 1856 for the 'reformation of penitents and preservation of girls of 16 and upwards from vice or danger'.

1885, December
Convent of the Good Shepherd
Bristol
All for Jesus
Dear Mrs. Hynes
 I am sorry to have kept you without news longer than I
intended being very busy. There is no improvement & at times our poor dear Sister is very suffering, which is the case this afternoon but I hope it will pass off as before, Though one never feels sure how much longer there may be when her sufferings increase. However the doctor said a few days ago that he had known a similar case in a girl of seventeen & she has recovered.

We must leave all in the hands of our dear Bd. Lord & He will do what is best for our dear Sister.

Please tell yr. Little daughter Nellie that S.M of S. Bertha was so pleased with her nice letter & thanks you for sending her brother's. I had written to him in her name & directed to Lancaster but I suppose it will follow him to Aldershot. The soldiers there have two priests.
Wishing you a Merry Christmas & wish love to all from our sisters.

I remain in the Sacred Heart
Very truly
S. Mary of the Good Shepherd ...

Poor Mary's sufferings grow worse although she has the attentions of a doctor and is in the close and constant care of her religious sisters. Had she still lived in Angel Meadow she could never have had such care.

1886, APRIL LETTER FROM SISTER MARY OF THE GOOD SHEPHERD

6 April 1886

All for the glory of God

Dear Mrs. Hynes
I must not leave you till the end of Lent without news of your dear daughter, but I am sorry I cannot to say she has made much progress. The discharge still continues tho she seems stronger & has gained flesh, but not as much as we hoped. I have therefore asked another doctor to call & he will come with our doctor in a few days & then we shall know if anything can be done. I hope you are better & that you will get quite well as the weather becomes milder.

D.J. Mary St. Bertha sends her love to you & her dear Sister & brother & hopes they pray for her & you also when you go to Holy Communion.

I remain in the Sacred Heart
Very truly
S. Mary of the good Shepherd ....

1886, July LETTER FROM SISTER MARY OF THE GOOD SHEPHERD

This came from Arnos Court which was a Good Shepherd Convent between 1851and 1948.

Convent of the Good Shepherd
Arno's Vale
Bristol
4 July 1886
I am very glad to cheer you by good news of our dear Sister who has taken a turn for the better which really looks like lasting improvement. The Doctor found her better in every way at his last visit & there has been further improvement since. She looks quite like her old self but of course extremely weak, & only gets from her bed to the sofa. You cannot be too sure but there is certainly great present improvement but we must leave the future in God's hands. I enclose some little things from S. M. Bertha for her little brother & sisters & she begs they will wear the D. Heart scapulars inside their clothes. The picture of the Cross is for yourself with her fond love & she hopes you are much better.

I was rather uneasy at Nellie's last letter speaking of you as very ill. Will you tell the dear child to let me know on a separate piece of paper what is the matter with you & if there is any danger as I will get the prayers of her Sisters for you, tho unless there was great danger, I do not want to tell S. Bertha. But I hope the good news will revive you. [Three words unclear here] .me in the Sacred Heart

Very truly
Sr. Mary of the Good Shepherd

We hope you have heard from George he wrote here last week & was well & hopeful that Sr. Bertha would get better. { Initials here}

These few letters make mention of injury, John's leg burn (industrial injury); Mary's illness (early deprivation affliction); and now Bridget (deprivation affliction). The sister superior holds out hope for Mary and expresses concern for Bridget's health even asking that her report on her health should be on a separate sheet of paper presumably so that Mary doesn't see it and worry.

The same month LETTER FROM SISTER MARY OF THE HOLY INNOCENTS

1886, July
Superior
Convent of the Good Shepherd
Arnos Vale
Bristol

14 July 1886

I am sure you will be anxious to hear how your dear daughter is going on. I am sorry to say this hot weather tries her very much & she is very suffering. The doctor does not now think there is much likelihood of her getting better as she has lost strength very much the last two months and cannot take as much nourishment as she did 3 months ago. She is however quite happy & resigned to God's will & the sister who nurses her is very kind to her & does all she can to relieve her sufferings. She is so very patient and good that we are all very proud of her, in fact I often
feel she is much too good for this world far more fit for heaven. You are indeed blessed to have such a child & I am sure if Our Lord takes her she will obtain many graces & blessings for you. She sends her love to you & her brothers and sisters & was much pleased to get Ellens letters & to hear you were better than when you wrote before. If she should get worse I would write to you at once.

Wishing you every blessing.
I remain
Yrs. Sincerely in Our Lord Sister M of the Holy Innocents Superior ...

There is nothing hopeful about Mary's affliction in this letter but there is praise about her patience in the face of suffering and some consolation in the mention of care from attentive sisters. Bridget Hynes is still unwell.

1886, October

George was promoted Lance Corporal on 11 October 1886. Here I give the contents of a letter home a few days after his promotion. Serving in Ireland seemed to have been classified as a home posting!

1886 LETTER FROM GEORGE TO HIS MOTHER

15 October 1886
Dear Mother
I hope you will forgive me for not writing before this as I have been anxious about you not writing (writing obscured)....you was ill till James Dowling (writing obscured)......told which put me about so I hope you will write soon & let me know how you are, as I am very Anxious. They would not send me out to India been such a good character so the Color Sergeant told me to put in for the stripe which I got. I'll not be able to come down till the 1ST. of January and it would cost me about £2-5-0 so I shall have to get my Christmas in the Army again. But it is a good job I hav'nt went to India so I will be able to see you & my dear Sisters & brothers again so I hope you will write As soon as you can & let me know how you are getting on so no more at present from

Your beloved son
L/Cpl G.Hynes
1311 "E" Company
4th. Kings' Own Regt
Buttevant
County Cork
Ireland

According to Lewis' Topographical Dictionary of 1837, the Buttevant barracks were "...an extensive range of buildings, occupying a spacious enclosed area of nearly 23 statute acres, divided into two quadrangles by the central range, in which is an archway surmounted by a cupola and affording communication between them". It lay to the north west of a solitary main street, a coach road. There would have been about 500 soldiers in Buttevant, 85% of them Protestant.

In the nineteenth century it was customary for Irish soldiers to serve in India but George did not want to go so far from his family so he did his best to avoid such a posting.

£2-5-0, two pounds five shillings, was a large sum in 1886-about almost 3 weeks' pay for a labourer and virtually unattainable for a young soldier. Soldiers were paid about one shilling a day, less stoppages, so that sum represented 45 weeks' pay for George.

1887 LETTER FROM SISTER SUPERIOR TO MARY'S MOTHER BRIDGET

Convent of the Good Shepherd, Hammersmith, London
28 February 1887

Dear Mrs. Hynes,

I believe you have been told that your dear Daughter, our Sister Mary of St. Bertha, was sent to us from our Convent near Bristol to see if this Doctor could do anything to cure her. He said from the first, he saw no hope, but she might live still a few weeks. She never got any better but last week she received the Holy Viaticum again. Yesterday she was carried to Mass. There was no change in her usual state only she did not seem to wish to get up this morning so she remained in bed & was sleeping quietly. She had her dinner as usual & just as the Angelus at twelve rang those were with her, saw she was dying. They ran for us to say the prayers, and also for our good Priest, but all was over before we got to the room without a struggle or a sigh. She looks beautiful, but it is necessary she should be buried immediately, so tomorrow she will be carried down into our little Church & after a night there, Mass & the Holy Office on Wednesday she will be taken to our other London Convent (for we may not be buried there now) and buried with our other sisters in the cemetery there: Mass is at Finchley. I have sent you a few little things she valued but if …….wish for let me know. And get all the prayers you can for her, for though she was very good one never knows if those we love may not still be helped by prayer. I will write to her Brother Corporal Hynes from whom she had a letter not long ago so I have his address. You must not fret for her she has been happy and a chosen soul and will .. now

Believe me, in union with the SS Hearts of Jesus & Mary
Yours truly Sr. Mary of S. Ignatius , Superior

This was the year the Artist Lawrence Stephen Lowry (1887-1976) was born in the Angel Meadow neighbourhood. His maternal grandparents lived on Oldham Road, close to Saint Michael's Flags. His grandfather was a moderately prosperous hatter). During his career, Lowry made several sketches and paintings of St. Michael and All Angels.

1887, February

Mary Connolly, Sr. Mary of St Bertha, first born child of Bridget by Patrick Connolly, died on 28 February 1887 in the Convent of the Good Shepherd.

A death certificate issued in the Fulham Registration Sub District of St. Paul, Hammersmith, in March 1887, confirms that Mary Connolly died on the twenty eighth of February 1887 at age 24. Her occupation was given as nun, daughter of Patrick Connolly (deceased) assistant at iron works. She died of a 'scrofular abdominal abcess' and Jane Shepherd of the Convent of the Good Shepherd, Hammersmith, was present at the death.

1887, March ANOTHER LETTER FROM SISTER SUPERIOR TO MARY'S MOTHER, BRIDGET

Convent of the Good Shepherd, Hammersmith, London

Dear Mrs. Hynes,

I have received your letter & send you a few more little things; but you must remember I sent you some, and nuns have not many possessions. She was very fond of the little statue of our Lady of Lourdes, and the Rosaries were always about her or in her hands. I sent her Brother her Imitation of Christ & some Agnus Dei she wore around her and sure she will pray for you. You will give something to her Sister will you not, and let me know that you receive all safe.

I am Very truly

Sr. Mary of St. Ignatius, Superior

Note by Ellen McCormick, descendant of Ellen Hynes from Angel Meadow: "The Sister Superior is called Sister Mary of St. Ignatius and her lay name was Jane Shepherd. The Sister's lay name appears on Mary's death certificate. I know she is the Sister Superior because I checked her name on the census. It was through this death certificate that I found out that Mary was a Connolly."

George gained his 3rd Class certificate of Education on the 14 March 1887. He was thus qualified to attain the rank of sergeant.

A SHORT BIOGRAPHY OF MARY CONNOLLY

In the year 2004 I communicated with the sister archivist of the Good Shepherd Sisters and I am grateful for her informative reply.

2004 LETTER FROM THE ARCHIVIST OF THE GOOD SHEPHERD SISTERS

(Although this letter is given here out of chronological sequence, it is a summary of Mary Connolly's life as a religious sister and therefore appropriately placed.)

Good Shepherd Sisters, Cranbrook Road, Staplehurst, Kent TN12 OER
Telephone and e mail addresses given …

14 October 2004
Dear Mr. Hynes,

Your request for information about your relative Mary Connolly, Sr. Mary of St Bertha, was sent on to me at the above address.

I am happy to put the following together for you from the records of the various Communities where Sister lived.
Mary Connolly was born in Manchester c.1862. I imagine it was between March and September but maybe you have something more specific? Her parents were Patrick Connolly and Bridget Tierney.

In May 1881 Mary entered the Novitiate of the Good Shepherd Sisters in Hammersmith. After four months as a Postulant she asked for and received the cream Habit of a Good Shepherd Novice on $_{25}$th September 1881. She was given the religious name Sr Mary of St Bertha. In the formal statement of freedom she stated that she was taking this step 'with the consent of my mother'.

Having completed the canonical 2 years' Novitiate and now age 21, Sr. Mary of St. Bertha made her solemn Profession on 26th. September 1883, received her first appointment, which was to join the Good Shepherd Community in Cardiff.

In the Annals of this Cardiff Community it is recorded that she 'endeared herself to everyone by her amiable, obliging and gentle manner. She was particularly respected by the women and girls in our care'. This latter point says a lot about her as the women and teenagers received into Good Shepherd Homes all had problems of some kind and were not always the easiest to deal with. Many had not been well treated by family or society and were placed in Good Shepherd Residential Homes for some sort of training and preparation for their future. Some went there directly from the Courts, having been given a 'Condition of residence in a place of correction' in preference to going to prison. Your relative, Sr Mary of St Bertha, obviously had a way of winning the confidence and respect of these disturbed but sometimes very hurt people.

She stayed at Cardiff for two years that is until 28 September 1885, when she moved to the Community in Bristol. She seemed to settle in well but soon displayed disquieting symptoms of the cruel disease which was finally to claim her at the age of 24. Initially she seemed to respond to treatment and for some months an encouraging improvement raised everyone's spirits but it did not last and it was decided to take her back to London for more specialised medical care.

On 31st. January 1887 accompanied by two Sisters and a friend of the Community, Sr. Mary of St Bertha was taken from the Good Shepherd Convent in Bristol to that of Hammersmith, where she had started her religious life. The following day a specialist, Mr. Barnes, came to see her. He withheld his diagnosis for three days, visiting her daily and carrying out various tests. The remedies provided gave her some relief and ensured that she had a good sleep every night. On the third day Mr. Barnes told the Superior that Sister was in 'a decline', as he had diagnosed the dreaded scrofula, TB of the lymph glands. At this stage Sister's mind became affected and she was quite confused at times. Everything humanly possible was done for her and it is recorded that she displayed a remarkable resignation, patience and gratitude throughout her illness. On 17 February she was well enough to receive the Sacrament of Holy Viaticum and even to walk along the corridor to the Tribune [an upstairs balcony within the Church] but that did not last for too long. It was obvious her condition was deteriorating.

On the 28 February she did not seem to be any worse, and had her usual small meal about 11.30 but shortly afterwards without any warning a great change came over her. The Sister-nurse called the Superior and other Sisters. They gathered hastily and prayed and sang at her bedside hoping that she could hear them. Within a few minutes and without struggle or any further apparent change, she slipped away before their eyes. It was shortly after 12.00 noon. She was 24 years of age.

Because of the nature of her illness it was deemed imperative that the funeral take place immediately. Sister was buried in the Convent cemetery in East Finchley, London.

In 1974 when most of the land surrounding the Finchley Convent was sold, the Sisters buried in that cemetery were transferred to our Convent cemetery here in Staplehurst and re-interred together. I do have some photographs of that communal grave but as our archives are in store at present I am unable to get at them. Meanwhile I do not want to delay sending this account of Sister but I assure you that I will send a photograph before too long.

With every good wish,

God bless,
Sr. Rosaria Kenny

1887, June
George gained his 2nd Class Certificate of Education on the 8 June, 1887 and on the 29 June, 1887 at age 18 he was promoted full corporal.

1887 LETTER FROM GEORGE TO HIS SISTER ELLEN

The letter heading was a regimental badge of the Kings Own Royal Lancaster Regiment.

22 September 1887
My Dearest Sister
I write you these few lines hopeing you are in good health as it leaves me at Present. I am alright & out of Hospital. Dear Sister I will send you a few shillings on the 8th. of next month & I will never forget the kindness you bestowed upon me I hope my Mother is in good health & as plenty of work & I am very glad to hear that Maggie as made a start & I hope she will keep it & I hope John Thomas is still going to school I am going to Killarney next month it is a fine place I suppose you have heard of that great riot at Mitchelstown* it is only six miles from our place & we have a company of soldiers & 1.000 ball ammunition with them & they say there will be more bloodshed before long. Dear Sister you can give my best respects to Pat & Mary Ellen Sullivan also Mr. & Mrs. Morris & Bella & Nelly Smith Jim Marshall & Tom Dillon so I must conclude by sending my best respects to yourself not forgetting my Mother , Maggie & john. I remain Your Ever loving brother G. Hynes
Corporal G. Hynes

B Company
1st. Royal Lancs Regt
Bullevant Ireland Forgive the scratching as I had a bad pen

* My note: August 9: During the 1887 riots at Mitchelstown, Ireland, three persons were killed & several injured by the military. It was thereafter known as the Mitchelstown massacre (1887). This was one of the all too many instances of Irish soldiers serving in British regiments killing other Irish!

1888, May GEORGE DEMOTED

On the 12 May 1888, George lost his corporal's stripes and spent 4 days, from the 13 May to the 16 May, in arrest for being drunk. It might have been close arrest, that is in the regimental guardroom or it might have been open arrest that is 'confined to barracks'. He was officially tried and reduced in rank on the 17 May and released from arrest. That may have happened in Buttevant or later in Dublin.

1889, March GEORGE SERVING IN DUBLIN MARRIES BRIDGET OWEN

The Barracks, later The Royal Barracks, were the oldest continuously occupied barracks in the world when the name was changed to Collins Barracks at the formation of the Irish Free State in 1922. In the 1880's, when George was stationed there the Commissioners of the War Office declared them to be dangerously inadequate and soldiers had died of diseases caught within those contaminated buildings. The letter date 4 March tells of George being in hospital so perhaps he had fallen victim to one of the a diseases actively infecting soldiers in those condemned barrack blocks.

George, born on 26 January 1869, was stationed at those Royal Barracks, Dublin when he married Bridget Owen, born 1868, a milliner, in Dublin, on 3 March 1889 in the Catholic Chapel of St. Michan. She lived in 20 Coleraine Street, just a couple of hundred yards north of the Inns Quay and only a street or two away from the barracks. Her father was William Owens, a painter, her mother Anne Owens. One may assume that during his recreational excursions from the Royal Barracks he must have met with and courted this Irish colleen. (This Bridget , wife of George, died on 7 February 1929 in Liverpool aged 61.)

1889, December BIRTH OF JOHN WILLIAM HYNES

John William Hynes, their first child, was born on the twenty eighth of December, 1889 in 22 Coleraine Street, Dublin, next door to his mother's parents, the Owens. In the years before the Great War, this person, my uncle John, Bridget's first born, an early member of the Liverpool Regiment Territorials attended parades in a drill hall. His service number, 163, was a very early one indeed. My grandmother Annie Doyle (nee McDonald) and my grandmother Bridget Hynes lived next door to each other in Vauxhall Road. They often stood outside their front doors at the top of the steps to chat and watch the passers-by. Bridget's eldest son, John, a snappy dresser, would often pass between them and walk downs the steps on his way out. In civvies he wore spats and carried a silver topped cane as he walked smartly along the road. Consequently the two mothers, both Irish wits, always referred to him as, 'The Toff'. He went on to serve the whole of the First World War on the Western Front.

CORRESPONDENCE CONTINUES

1890, March

1890 LETTER FROM BRIDGET HYNES TO HER SISTER-IN-LAW ELLEN: GEORGE IN HOSPITAL: NEW BABY, JOHN WILLIAM FLOURISHING

20 Coleraine St

Mar 4Th. 1890

I received your kind & welcome Letter & is sorry to hear that your Mother is so ill. But please God it will not be long before she is well. The reason I delayed your letter was I was waiting to see George on Sunday to see had he anything to Say. He is very sorry to hear about his Mother & he is greatly fretted about her. He told me to tell you that he has no way of writing to you or he would have wrote long go he is not Better yet he is afraid that he will be in hospital for another 3 Weeks. Myself and the Baby is getting on well he is stout and strong I am hardly able to mind him. I am glad to hear that Maggie & John Thomas is well not forgetting yourself. My Father and Maria is very sorry to hear about yor Mother they also sends their Best respects to all the family Maria Says to excuse her for not sending her Photo for she does not like it. But she will get another one taken & send it you. I went to get the childs photo taken By himself & he was to young & I had to get it taken along with him & I was not intended to get it taken with the dress it had on me. When Georg is able to come out we intend to get the 3 of us on this one card.

No more at present from your affectionate Sister=in =Law B Hynes
Please Answer it again Sunday if you can I want to have word for George how your Mother is.

1890, October
LETTER FROM/ FOR BRIDGET HYNES, THE YOUNGER, TO HER SISTER-IN-LAW

28 October 1889. The original looks as if it was written by someone on behalf of Bridget who dictated and signed it. The writer made a mistake with the year. This must have been 1890 not 1889!

Dear Sister in Law
I new take the pluser of answering your kind letter and was glad to find you all in good health as it leaves us all at present thank god for it Dear Sister in law you must excuse me for not writing sooner as I was waiting to get George out of the Armly and we have good news he has got out to the Armly Reserve as we will be over soon new I wood like to have the pluser of seen you before you go Away as George was telling us. Dear Sister in law I was very sorry to hear of the trouble at home and all so about your Ant being ill hoping by this time it will find her in good health Johney william is eable to dance and sing as good as the father I will think the time will never come till I go over to see yous give my kind love to Mother ellen allso John thomas not forget mrs.Smyth So now I will conclud with kind love to all.
So no more
at present from
your loven Sister in law

B. Hynes not forgeting a few XXXXXXXX

GEORGE LEAVES THE REGULAR ARMY AND CONTINUES IN THE RESERVES

George was released from the regulars and transferred to the Reserves on the twenty-eighth of October, 1890 at his own request in accordance with Army Regulations 4-136. Perhaps George used his mother's illness among other matters to gain his release from regular army service.

1890, March
LETTER FROM BRIDGET HYNES TO HER SISTER-IN-LAW ELLEN: GEORGE LEAVES HOSPITAL

20 Coleraine St
Mar 13th. 1890

Dear Ellen
I received your kind & welcome letter & is glad to hear that your Mother is getting strong again. George is alright now thank God. He expects to be out next week & he is glad to hear that his Mother is getting Better & he sends his kind Love to all & he says not to forget to drown the Shamrock. I am glad to hear that you were pleased with my Photo & the childs. Give my kind Love to your Mother & not forgetting Maggie & John Thomas also yourself Also my Father & Maria also yourself is glad To hear that you are all enjoying the Best of Health. This Photo is the one that Maria got taken she does not like it a couple of her comrade Girls made her put her hair up on top and it makes her look to old looking she generally wear her hair hanging. But she will get another one taken. I hope you will share this with Mrs. Smith & Maria says there is a little piece there for Tommy Dillon. Excuse me for not writing to you Before this. I was waiting to send all together. When you get the Shamrock Put it in Water & shake agrain of salt in the Water & that will keep it fresh. George does have great sport with the child when I bring him up to see him & he knows him real well & he is always laughing at him. No more at Present From your Affectionate Sister=in=Law B. Hynes

John William sends these few xxxxxxxxxx to his Grand Ma & also his Aunt and Little Uncle & also remember me to Mrs. Smith.

The handwriting is different on each of the letters from young Bridget so as likely as not she couldn't write and had two different persons write at her dictation.

1890, December
DEATH OF BRIDGET HYNES, GEORGE'S MOTHER

Ellen McCormick referring to a copy of a registration of death tells us that Bridget Hynes, George's mother, died on the seventeenth of December 1890 in the house where her husband died five years previously, 28 Style St. Bridget was 45 and she died of catarrhal double pneumonia. Her son, George was present. At the time that district of Ancoats, not to be wondered at, was the death black spot of Manchester if not of all England. His mother died a few months after his release from the army. He became a Reservist returning to serve as a sergeant then warrant officer during the Boer War.

Ancoats was the death black spot of Manchester and that is where George's mother died. The death rate of Angel Meadow, based upon calculations for the year 1888-89-90 was 50.9 per thousand per annum. The average for all England during the same period was less than 19. Bridget had fallen victim to the miasmas of Angel Meadow and Style Street harboured the worst of them. The Street harboured not only deadly diseases but deadly criminals such as Bob Horridge previously mentioned as one who leapt into the Irk. The detective Jerome Caminada wrote: "On his release from penal servitude, "Bob" again went into business for himself in Style Street, Rochdale Road. He was very successful, and soon bought up only and a long cart with low sides, which is necessary for him to convey his goods to the various wholesale houses where he did business. It was very well known that when "Bob" was not in prison robberies occurred more frequently in Manchester than when he was confined."

GEORGE AND BRIDGET HYNES

The 5 April 1891 census showed George Hynes, 24 yrs., his wife Bridget 23 yrs., and baby son, John William, 1 yr., living at 70 Nelson Street, Manchester. George gave his employment as Railway Porter. John Thomas Hynes, age 14, was also living with the family and was employed as an apprentice slipper maker but he died that same year on the 12 August in the Clinical Hospital, Manchester of bronchopneumonia (11 days) & emphysema (2 days). His sister Ellen Hynes, of 23 Nicholas Street reported the death. Under 'occupation' is written, son of John Hynes (deceased), General Labourer. Young John was yet another victim of the poisonous Meadow.

Nelson Street was far enough away from Style Street for George and his wife to feel they had left that terrible place behind. They must have left Angel Meadow after his mother's death there in 1890. Margaret Hynes was living in number 1 Style Street as a lodger. She was employed as a stay maker for dresses. (Ellen McCormick could not find Ellen Hynes on the 1891 census.)

George's 1891 home, rented rooms, was only a few doors away from number 62 Nelson Street where Emmeline Pankhurst, the leading suffragette was born 33 years earlier. Number 70 Nelson Street survives today as the Pankhurst Centre open for public viewing.

In addition to her still famous activities in the Suffragette movement, Votes for Women, after meeting and befriending the socialist politician Keir Hardie in 1888 Pankhurst helped found the Independent Labour Party and took part in the distribution of food to the poor through the Committee for the Relief of the Unemployed. In 1894 she became Poor Law Guardian in Chorlton-on-Medlock. After visiting a Manchester workhouse she wrote: *"The first time I went into the place I was horrified to see little girls seven and eight years old on their knees scrubbing the cold stones of the long corridors ... bronchitis was epidemic among them most of the time ... I found that there were pregnant women in that workhouse, scrubbing floors, doing the hardest kind of work, almost until their babies came into the world ... Of course the babies are very badly protected ... These poor, unprotected mothers and their babies I am sure were potent factors in my education as a militant."*

1891 THE CENSUS AND RERUM NOVARUM

The year 1891 was not only the time of a census but it also was the year when Pope Leo XIII signed and issued the social encyclical Rerum Novarum, The Workers' Charter, the first mile stone, on the road of Catholic social teaching. Its very title is taken from the first two words of the Latin text translating as ' of revolutionary changes'. The title was apt, following as it did the Communist Manifesto of 1848. This 'charter' condemned the excesses of both socialism and laissez-faire capitalism whilst defending the rights of workers to form unions and the rights of property owners. The rights and duties of the family over the State were defended whilst people were urged to accept their lot since hard work and suffering were part of the human condition. Whilst asking the poor to be patient the encyclical asked industrialists to be more caring in their treatment of workers. "Wherefore, since wage workers are numbered among the great mass of the needy, the State must include them under its special care and foresight."

Fearing revolution which only brought more misery and death, the Pope sought stability by insisting that the State should defend the rights of people without property as a matter of justice. Oppressed workers, above all, ought to be liberated from the savagery of greedy men, who inordinately use human beings as things for gain.

The encyclical went on to condemn excessive toil which dulls the spirit and which brings exhaustion that crushes the body. The working energy of a man, like his entire nature, is circumscribed by definite limits beyond which it cannot go.

That was the condition of workers living in Angel Meadow a place like so many others where the state should have intervened, as the encyclical proposed, to ensure the workers received a 'just wage' enabling them to live in frugal comfort. The people of Angel Meadow and others trying to survive in similar industrial ghettoes were still a long way away from frugal comfort.

Among those who cared in 1893 Angel Meadow was still being cited as a terrible blighted place. For example the December 10 1893 issue of The Spy treated its readers to: "The dreary wastes of Angel Meadow. Down Angel Street, with its pestiferous lodging houses, with its bawds and bullies, its thieves and beggars, one had need to visit such a place when the sun is high in the heavens. When night falls I had rather enter an enemy's camp during the time of war than venture near such dens of infamy and wretchedness, but the poor live here and die here."

MORE OBSERVATIONS ON ANGEL MEADOW

.
In October 1899, many flagstones were stolen thus contributing to further deterioration of the neighbourhood. St Michael's Church was eventually abandoned becoming structurally unsafe and eventually demolished in 1935. Georgian houses, factories, including the Co-op's cigarette factory, and the Victorian back-to-back houses were also torn down.

EMINENT PEOPLE WHO KNEW THE NEIGHBOURHOOD

The great social novelist, Charles Dickens once worked briefly in the nearby Meadow's Booth's warehouse. It is thought that his experiences of the dreadful slum conditions there may have influenced his novel, Hard Times set as it was in a fictitious Victorian industrial Coketown, a generic Northern English mill-town. Dickens commented that the ragged schools run by evangelical groups were "not sufficiently secular, presenting too many religious mysteries and difficulties, to minds not sufficiently prepared for their reception".

The maternal grandparents of the now acclaimed painter of working class Manchester, L.S. Lowry lived on Oldham Road close to Angel Meadow scene of some of his works such Britain at Play and The Steps, Irk Place,1928 which recently raised £713,250 at auction. Lowry provided many a visual record of the area, including his View of the Nation (1936).

Winston Churchill visited the Charter Street Ragged School when he stood as a Conservative candidate in Oldham.

Jerome Caminada who was born in Deansgate, Manchester in 1844, to an Irish mother and an Italian father became a high-ranking detective in Manchester police force said to be Manchester's very own Sherlock Holmes, worked in the area. His account of his life in '25 Years of Detective Life – a fascinating account of crime in Victorian Manchester' is a fine piece of social history.

Ethnic solidarity was such there among the Irish that Joseph Sadler Thomas, Deputy Constable of the Township of Manchester wrote: "In Angel Meadow, or Little Ireland, if a legal execution of any kind is to be made, either for rent or debt, or for taxes to the officer who served the process almost always applies to me for assistance to protect him; and, in affording protection, my officers after maltreated by Brickbats and other missiles". Cited by Busteed and Hodgson in Angel Meadow: a Study of the Geography of Irish settlement in Mid-Nineteenth Century Manchester

GEORGE AND HIS FAMILY MOVE TO LIVERPOOL

1895, June
Although George was still living in Manchester in 1891 by 1895 and possibly earlier he had moved with his family into Liverpool, into the district of Everton which was also an area populated by Roman Catholic Irish migrants. He then began work at Crosfields Sugar Refinery, one of about half a dozen in that district on and near Vauxhall Road and some thirty six such refineries operating in the city.

By the time his Army Reserve service expired on 23 October 199, he and Bridget were parents of John William, born in Ireland, George Hynes, junior, James Edward Hynes and   Richard Francis Hynes. Other later   children were Margaret, Mary, Thomas and Francis .Some months after my father Richard was born on 21 April 1899 , George re-enlisted in the Reserves signing on with the King's Own and serving with the Colours under Authority Number 40116/6707, as a Warrant Officer i.e. Sergeant Major   in South Africa. The 2nd Battalion of the King's Own Royal

Lancaster Regiment served in the South African War as part of the Lancashire Brigade. George took part in the South Africa Campaign between 24 Sept 1900 and 20 June 1901, for 1 year and 117 days. The Army Record says he was paid the South Africa War Gratuity which for someone with rank was probably a notable sum. He continued serving at home in the Reserves between 21 June 1901 and 15 April 1903. Altogether he served 16 years and 174 days in the regular and reserve army.

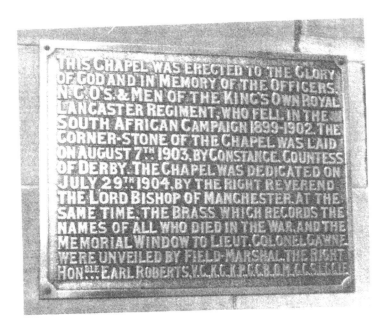

Commemorative plaque in the Regimental Chapel, Lancaster.

He gained the Queens South Africa Campaign Medal with clasps for the Orange Free State, Transvaal & Battle of Laing's Nek 1901. In May 1900 Boer forces occupied the mountain pass of Laing's Nek, where their predessors had held off the British in the First Boer War in 1881. George must have been in an action which re took the position in an assault on 12 June.

I think he was probably recommended as a time keeper at Crosfields Sugar Refinery, Vauxhall Road, Liverpool on the strength of his army experience and terminal rank, possibly by an ex-officer who knew him. The original sugar refinery in Vauxhall Road, Liverpool, started by George Crosfield of Warrington went into liquidation and closed down in 1907 when

George Hynes was working there. That mill was closed but Crosfield's own sons continued to prosper. His son Joseph Crosfield of Bank Quay Works, Warrington UK traded in soaps and perfumes including the famous Erasmic for which Crosfield received a Royal Warrant in 1905 from Edward VII.

All that was left of Crosfields Mill in the 1950's was this silo. In the early twentieth century there were tall Edwardian style houses on either side in one of which the mill manager George Hynes lived with his family.

George became foreman then manager and director of Crosfield Mill.

Some 800 men were put out of work in the Vauxhall Road refinery but George Hynes, a former time keeper had been kept on as caretaker while the owners planned its future. Mr. Job, nephew of Crosfield and an accountant, decided to take over the mill and he and George began running it an oil cake cattle feed mill after appropriate renovations. George became foreman and eventually works manager of the new Crosfields Oil and Cake Mills, 388 Vauxhall Road, Liverpool and the family moved into and lived in converted rooms within the factory building eventually moving into a nearby house number 370 Vauxhall Road.

Crosfields prospered despite the rivalry presented by the larger Bibby's and other cattle food manufacturers operating in the same neighbourhood. Interestingly according to local informal history both companies preferentially employed Catholic workers.

The four older sons of Bridget and George served in the First Great War. **John served with the Liverpool Regiment throughout the whole war ending up as a Warrant Officer Instructor at the Bisley School of Musketry.**

Richard served first with Manchesters then with the Lancashire Fusiliers. He served throughout World War Two in the Royal Air Force as did his brother George who had served as a Flight Sergeant engineer in X Flight in support of Lawrence of Arabia.

James Edward served first with the Connaught Rangers and then with the Inniskillings when wounded and captured and dying of the Great Flu in November 1918 in a German POW camp.

George's sister, Margaret, who never married also left Manchester for Liverpool.

George's sister, Ellen, whose great granddaughter Ellen McCormick has the original letters.

GEORGE JUNIOR 'RESCUED' LAWRENCE OF ARABIA

Those four grandsons of the migrant Irish couple, John and Bridget Hynes who went on to serve in the British Armed Forces during World War One epitomised the net contribution migrants from the maligned Angel Meadow made to their birth nation, England. The grudging question: What have the immigrants ever done for us? is still being asked by xenophobes today as there were during the influx of the Irish in the nineteenth century. The answer is the same today as it ever was, They contribute to the common good. Recent research tends to report favourably in monetary terms rather than in terms of benefits to the gene pool and civic contributions, service to the nation, but all agree that migrants have a positive impact. For example economists at University College,

London, discovered that they pay out far more in taxes than they receive in state benefits and the migrants bring in intellectual gifts, they themselves!

One of those grandsons of John Hynes, George Samuel Hynes, born in 1895, went on to serve in the Royal Flying Corps and actually rescued the great Lawrence of Arabia when marooned in the desert.

George born in Liverpool became a marine engineer, joined the Royal Flying Corps at the beginning of the First World War and became an RFC flight engineer servicing the aircraft of a secret X Flight providing close support to Lawrence of Arabia. His exploits appear in my book, 'Lawrence of Arabia's Secret Air Force: based on the Diary of Flight Sergeant George Hynes' published by Pen and Sword.

" X Flight was designated the task of giving close air support to the desert army formed and commanded by Lawrence of Arabia. It flew from advanced desert landing grounds on reconnaissance, liaison, bombing and ground attack missions. The existence and deeds of the flight were kept secret, so much so that even the RFC Paymaster was unaware of their existence. George Hynes was an aircraft mechanic and became responsible for keeping the flight's somewhat elderly aircraft airworthy whilst working in the most difficult desert conditions on hastily constructed landing strips and living and working under canvas in temperatures that froze at night and rose to 100 degrees plus at noon. His diary gives a clear insight into the conditions endured, the actions that took place and the many almost insurmountable problems that occurred as they followed Lawrence s steady advance against the numerically superior Turkish Army and Air Force. George personally encountered Lawrence on many occasions and maintained contact with him after the war. The diary is supported with the Flights weekly operational records, perspectives of the battle scenarios and other background information."

GEORGE 'RESCUES' LAWRENCE AND BORTON HIS PILOT

In his own words George recounted an incident which happened in April 1918:

"I was told by Captain Furness-Williams, my commanding officer, that the pilot of the visiting aircraft had reported Lawrence stranded on Sinai. His machine had made a forced landing because of engine trouble and I had to go out in the visiting aircraft and get him safely to Aquaba. I took tools, funnel and four gallons of aviation spirit.

Our aircraft put down on a sandy plateau and there was Lawrence. He was standing with his pilot near the stranded machine at the only time I ever saw him in a British khaki uniform. Lawrence gave us his unperturbed smile although I thought he looked very comical in that oversized uniform with no belt, wearing a flattened cap looking like a shop dummy wearing an off-the-peg uniform. He wore that uniform for no longer than about ten hours before discarding it in favour of a white cloak from Feisal, and as we heard equivalent to a status of a Prince of Mecca.

I put the defect right, tested the engine, put it into trim and passed it OK. The take-off was proving to be a very difficult task owing to the very soft sandy conditions and a limited area for the run up. Borton made three cautious attempts but had to pull up each time just short of a sump hole because falling into that would have been disastrous. He would have crashed with T. E. sitting just behind the engine.

I realised that T. E. must be got back safely because the Arabs would never have succeeded without him. Only Lawrence was able to bond them together in a common cause.

I stopped all further attempts until I toured the area and had selected a fresh run fit for take-off. I then advised my pilot to hang on to the wings, I on the port, he on the starboard wing. Borton was advised to rev up the engine to full throttle while we pushed on the machine until I gave the word. Also Borton decided to use a little rudder to allow for the propeller torque to keep the machine on a straight course and to prevent a loss of speed during take-off. That time Colonel Borton managed the take-off [and] much to my relief the machine became airborne." George then climbed back into the Flight's BE2c for a journey back to their desert airstrip.

Younger siblings of George Samuel were: Thomas Patrick Hynes 1902; in 1904 Mary Hynes (Regrettably she died shortly after marriage in 1927 without offspring); 1906 Margaret Hynes and the youngest in 1908, Francis Hynes.

Bridget Hynes, mother of the above, died young at aged 45 , like many another Bridget from Angel Meadow, but her genes   are to be found in her descendants among whom are professional , skilled , semi –skilled and unskilled people living in Britain, Canada, America, Australia, New Zealand, Hong Kong and Africa. Some have doctorates, some have Masters' degrees and some have degrees in law, in education, in philosophy, chemistry, theology, drama, economics, town planning, geography, engineering, education, sociology and so on. Others are or have been: priest, solicitor, lecturer, town planner, soldiers, airline pilot, teachers, students, nurses, tobacco farmers, electricians, cabinet maker, roofer, labourers, carpenter, housewives, businessmen, barbers, technicians, dog groomers, shop assistants, unemployed, retired, traffic managers and so on. In other words her descendants are to be found among a whole cross section of human enterprise- or none! I know of no convicts among them! Some are Catholics, some Buddhists, some atheists, some agnostics, some Protestants, many religiously indifferent and I dare say their levels of moral rectitude are spread over the whole normal curve of distribution.

After his wife's death in1929 George, then mill manager at Crosfields, married for a second time. When he died in 1942 he owned 5 well-appointed houses, very much superior to the ones he grew up in and he left a considerable sum of money to his widow and children.

Today Angel Meadow has once again been greened after its slums and industrial intruders have gone over the course of a century and more but it still manages to provide murder and mystery. In January 2010 builders working on the Co-op's new headquarters near Angel Meadow discovered the remains of a woman who was thereafter called the Angel of the Meadow. Forensic examination concluded that she had suffered fractured jaw, neck, collarbone and nose before death. Ongoing DNA work is trying to establish the identity of this woman whose dead body had been covered over by pieces of carpet. She is believed to have been killed between 1975 and 1988 but her identity and circumstances of her murder remain a mystery.

Here extracts from the website Friends of Angel Meadow : http://www.friends-of-angel-meadow.org/page2.htm illustrate the sterling work accomplished by the members in restoration and commemoration of the area.

"In 1999, the park was awarded a National Lottery Heritage grant to regenerate the neglected space for the benefit of a new residential community of Angel Meadow and challenge them to promote the history of the area."

"In 2004, the Friends of Angel Meadow (FOAM) formed to campaign for the park's continued redevelopment and since then considerable money has been raised through grants and Manchester City Council interest. This led to the renovation and re-landscaping of the park transforming it into a green retreat from the bustle of the city."

Membership of the Friends of Angel Meadow is free and its website fascinating; http://www.friends-of-angel-meadow.org/

APPENDIX

THE MANCHESTER ANGEL

It's coming down to Manchester to gain my liberty,
I met a pretty young doxy and she seemed full of glee.
Yes, I met a pretty young doxy, the prettiest ever I see.
At the Angel Inn in Manchester, there is the girl for me.

Then early next morning, just at the break of day,
I went to my love's bedside, my morning vows to pay.
I hugged her, I cuddled her, I bade her to lie warm;
And she said: "My jolly soldier, do you mean me any harm?'

"To mean you any harm, my love, is a thing that I would scorn.
If I stopped along with you all night, I'd marry you in the morn.
Before my lawful officer, my vows I will fulfil."
Then she said, "My jolly soldier, you may lie as long as you will.'

Our rout came on the Thursday, on the Monday we marched away.
The drums and fifes and bugles so sweetly did play.
Some hearts they were merry, but mine was full of woe.
She says: "May I go along with you? " "Oh no, my love, oh no."

"If you should stand on sentry go, on a cold and bitter day,
Your colours they would go, love, and your beauty would decay
If I saw you handle a musket, love, it would fill my heart with woe
So stay at home, dear Nancy." But still she answered, "No!"

"I'll go down to your officer, and I'll buy your discharge,
Ten guineas I'll surrender if they'll set you at large.
And if that will not do my love, along with you I'll go,
So will you take me with you now?" And still I answered: "No."

"I'll go down in some nunnery and there I'll end my life.
I'll never have no lover now, nor yet become a wife.
But constant and true-hearted, love, for ever I'll remain,
And I never will get married till my soldier comes again!'

Printed in Great Britain
by Amazon